LEFT: Dave Grohl, Kurt Cobain and Krist Novoselic: Nirvana in Germany, November 12, 1991.

THIS IS A CARLTON BOOK

This edition first published in Great Britain in 2016 by
Carlton Books
An imprint of the Carlton Publishing Group
20 Mortimer Street
London W1T 3JW

Copyright © Carlton Books Limited 2011, 2016

A CIP catalogue for this book is available from the British
Library.

ISBN 978-1-78097-770-6

Printed in China

The content of this book previously appeared in
Treasures of Nirvana

10 9 8 7 6 5 4 3 2 1

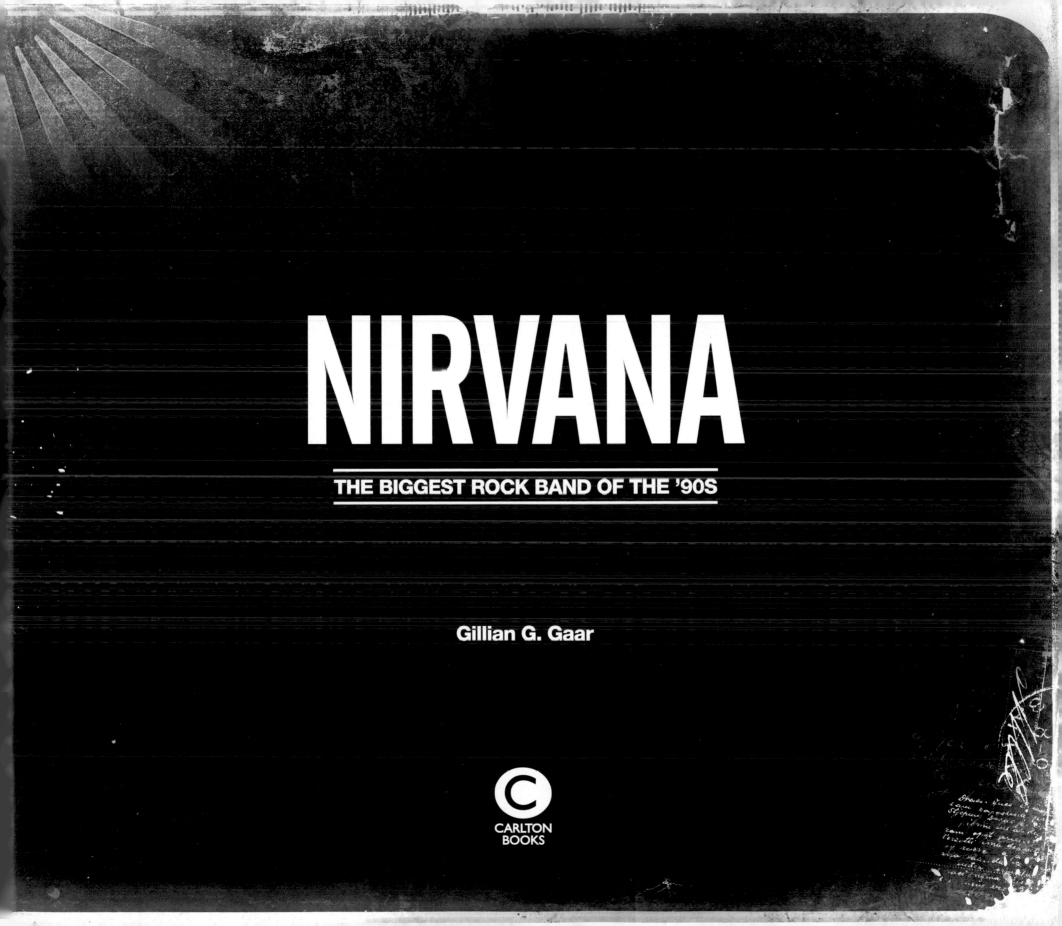

NIRVANA

THE BIGGEST ROCK BAND OF THE '90S

Gillian G. Gaar

CARLTON BOOKS

CONTENTS

INTRODUCTION

On April 24, 1988, a trio from Aberdeen, Washington, played one of their first shows in Seattle at one of the few clubs in the city that welcomed bands who played original music, The Vogue. More people were familiar with the group as being friends of another band from the same area, The Melvins, than they were with the fact that Kurt Cobain, Krist Novoselic, and Dave Foster were in a band in their own right - one who'd only recently settled on a final name: Nirvana.

Cobain was so nervous before the show he threw up. The band's unease was also apparent on stage. Photographer Charles Peterson, who was already documenting the burgeoning scenes for local Seattle records labels like Sub Pop, was one of those in attendance who remained unimpressed. "I had my camera there and I didn't bother to take pictures," he recalls. "I just thought, 'This is a joke. This is not going to go anywhere.'" Aware that the group was about to record for Sub Pop, Peterson approached the label's co-founder, Jonathan Poneman, who was also at the show, and said, "Jonathan – are you sure you want to sign these guys?"

Poneman was sure, though by the time Nirvana entered the studio to record their first record for Sub Pop that June, Foster would be replaced by Chad Channing on drums. Two years later, Channing would be replaced by Dave Grohl. A year after that, Nirvana would release their major label debut, *Nevermind*. And by January 1992, *Nevermind* would be the best selling album in the US, putting Nirvana on top of the Billboard charts.

It was an incredible rise, especially for a band from an area of the US that was then not particularly well known. Nor was Nirvana the first alternative rock band from the Pacific Northwest to be signed to a major label. But it was Nirvana's success that helped put the region on the map, and the band's success wasn't just musical. 1991, when *Nevermind* was released, wasn't just "the year punk broke" (as the title of Dave Markey's documentary of the 1991 European summer rock festival season, which featured Nirvana alongside groups like Sonic Youth and Babes In Toyland, put it). It marked a cultural shift that momentarily placed Seattle, and the Pacific Northwest, at the center of the pop culture universe. There were certainly times over the next few years when the attention got out of hand, as when the mainstream media ran photo spreads promoting something called "grunge fashion" (which didn't exist – really). But the more important element was the realization that over the preceding decade, a new generation had been steadily carving out a place for themselves, creating a music scene that wasn't beholden to corporate machinations but was truly grassroots.

Of course, the corporations soon moved in. To some, the high water mark of the Seattle scene came in 1990, before the major labels had skimmed off the cream of the crop, and signed the area's best bands. And certainly, with regard to the sense of freewheeling camaraderie that had existed between the bands and their audiences, this was true. There was a lack of self-consciousness in the scene that disappeared when Vogue began featuring models wearing long-sleeved plaid shirts not made out of flannel, but stone-washed silk.

But the music – "grunge" – has left behind a lasting legacy. Nirvana didn't invent grunge any more than The Beatles created the "Mersey Beat" (that honor probably goes to the Melvins). But as the first band from the region to attain mammoth success, they remain its standard bearers. And far from being "slackers," Cobain, Novoselic, and Grohl worked hard at their craft. Cobain, Nirvana's main songwriter, wrote songs that expressed the alienation and rage felt by others in his generation, leavened by a dose of sarcasm and self-deprecation, while Nirvana's live shows were joyous spectacles that had the band reveling in the sheer delight of being able to make as much noise as possible.

Kurt Cobain wouldn't live to see how the music he created went on to inspire others. As Nirvana's fame escalated, so did Cobain's drug habit, worsening to the point where he took his own life in April 1994. But those who focus on Cobain's death miss what is truly important about Nirvana's story. Quite simply, they created great music, from the raw roughness of *Bleach*, to the sublime grunge-pop melodicism of *Nevermind*, to the righteous fury of *In Utero*. Songs like 'Floyd The Barber,' 'About A Girl,' 'Sliver,' 'Smells Like Teen Spirit,' 'Lithium,' 'Heart-Shaped Box,' and 'Scentless Apprentice' touched on a myriad of emotions and contradictory feelings, with music that was alternately beautiful and harsh – often in the same song. Cobain was never able to resolve his own contradictions, but he never stopped trying to express his feelings about them; one of his last known songs, 'Do Re Mi,' later included on the posthumously released box set *With The Lights Out*, shows that his musical gifts never left him.

Nirvana's music is all we have left. This is their story.

Gillian G. Gaar, Seattle

THE EARLY YEARS

Though Nirvana was described as being part of the "Seattle Scene" of grunge bands when *Nevermind* topped the album charts in 1992, their story actually began 100 miles from the largest city in Washington State, in Aberdeen. Located in the southwestern corner of the state, Aberdeen was founded in 1884, named after the city of Aberdeen, Scotland. Like its Scots counterpart, Aberdeen is located at the mouth of two rivers – the Chehalis and the Wishkah. The town's first sawmill was built in 1894, and logging quickly became the primary industry; at one point there were nearly 40 mills in the region (including those in the neighboring towns of Hoquiam and Cosmopolis).

In the 1930s, Aberdeen's population was around 26,000; by the end of the century, that number had dropped to 16,000. The decline was due largely to the disappearance of jobs, as over-foresting led to the curtailing of the local timber industry in the 1980s. But all that lay ahead when Kurt Cobain was born at Aberdeen's Grays Harbor Community Hospital in 1967. As noted in Charles Cross' biography of Cobain, *Heavier Than Heaven*, the Vietnam War abroad and social unrest at home might have created turmoil elsewhere in the US, "but apart from the occasional news dispatch, Aberdeen felt more like 1950s America." *The Sound Of Music* had been playing at a movie house in Hoquiam for over a year; the area's local drive-in was showcasing the fun-in-the-sun antics of *The Girls On The Beach*.

Cobain was first child of Don and Wendy Cobain. The family first lived in Hoquiam, where Don worked at the local Chevron station, and moved to Aberdeen in 1969; Cobain's sister Kim was born in 1970. Cobain's interest in the arts was evident at a young age, and his skill at drawing led his family to keep him well stocked in art supplies. "It kind of got crammed down his throat," his mother later told author Michael Azerrad. "Every present was a paintbrush or an easel. We kind of almost killed it for him." Nonetheless, drawing and painting remained one of Cobain's primary interests throughout his life.

Cobain's other main interest was music. A few relatives on his mother's side dabbled in music; one uncle played in a local outfit called the Beachcombers, and his Aunt Mari played guitar in area clubs. Cobain grew up listening to the sounds of Top 40 pop radio, artists like the Beatles (a particular favorite), the Monkees, and the Byrds. The first instrument he gravitated to was the drums, which he later played in the school band.

Cobain recalled his early childhood as "blissful times." But that bliss was shattered after his ninth birthday when his parents divorced in 1976; in future interviews Cobain frequently mentioned how the divorce made him feel ashamed and worthless. "It was traumatic for Kurt, as he saw everything he trusted in – his security, family, and his own maintenance – unravel in front of his eyes," Aunt Mari told Charles Cross.

Cobain initially lived with his mother then moved in with his father, by then living in Montesano, a small town 11 miles from Aberdeen, where his own parents lived. In 1978, Don married a woman who had two children from a

RIGHT: In 2005, Aberdeen, Washington's "Welcome" sign was amended with a second sign bearing the name of a Nirvana song.

Welcome to Aberdeen

Come As You Are

previous marriage; the couple soon had a son of their own. Though at first Cobain was seemingly happy in the new family unit, as he entered his teens he became increasingly resentful, and when he was 15, he moved out. Cobain stayed with various family members; by the time he finally left Aberdeen in 1987, he'd lived in numerous households, none of them for longer than a year.

Music provided the one constant in his life. Along with the drums, Cobain also began developing an interest in the guitar. At age 8, his Aunt Mari had given him a cheap Hawaiian guitar and matching amp (some accounts say this guitar belonged to his father); when he turned 14 in 1981, he received a more professional (though still inexpensive) instrument for his birthday, a Lindell electric. He carried the guitar with him everywhere, spent hours practicing, and was soon writing his own songs. At the end of 1982, he traveled to Seattle, where his Aunt Mari had moved, and

recorded his first known demo on her 4-track recorder. He called the resulting tape "Organized Confusion," and the music made an impression on his friends, most of whom were more interested in covering popular songs of the day than writing their own material.

Cobain's musical tastes were also developing. Though he always retained a fondness for the Beatles, and cheesy pop songs (ABBA would later be a tour bus favorite), he was also keeping up with newer, harder acts, like Aerosmith, Queen, and Journey. In a profile of him in his school paper, he cited Electric Light Orchestra. and Meatloaf as favorites. He took guitar lessons for a brief period; his teacher, Warren Mason, upgraded his guitar to an Ibanez, and taught his eager pupil how to play such hard rock classics as Led Zeppelin's 'Stairway To Heaven' and AC/DC's 'Back In Black.'

LEFT: Kurt Cobain's childhood home in Aberdeen.

BELOW: This Aberdeen house (since demolished), where Kurt Cobain briefly lived in 1986–87. was where Nirvana's first rehearsals were held.

On March 29, 1983, Cobain attended his first big rock concert: Sammy Hagar and Quarterflash at the Seattle Center Coliseum. But his tastes in music were about to undergo a dramatic shift in a few months time. That summer, he witnessed his first show by the Melvins, a punk rock group that had formed right on his doorstep, in Montesano. The three piece band (then made up of Roger "Buzz" Osborne on guitar, Matt Lukin on bass, and Mike Dillard on drums) played an impromptu show in the parking lot of the local Thriftway grocery store, and Cobain was hooked. "This is what I was looking for," he later wrote in his journal. In the liner notes for a collection of 1983 demos, Osborne would later write: "Punk rock changed everything. It was a life-saving world unto itself, completely outside of the nine circles of hayseed hell that was my daily existence." It was a sentiment that Cobain could readily identify with.

Dillard was later replaced by Dale Crover, who lived in Aberdeen, and rehearsals moved to his parents' house. Cobain was quick to join the little group of followers who hung out at the house to watch the Melvins rehearse, one of whom was Krist Novoselic, a 6'7" first-generation Croatian, who'd spent his childhood in the suburbs of Los Angeles.

Like Cobain, Novoselic was initially interested in the pop music he heard on AM radio; when his father purchased a radio that could pick up FM stations, his tastes broadened to Led Zeppelin, Aerosmith, and Black Sabbath. When the family moved to Aberdeen, where Novoselic's father had relatives, in 1979, he felt a profound sense of culture shock, initially unable to find friends with common interests. "Music was so important to me and I was just way ahead," he later recalled. "Like, they were laughing at Aerosmith, but in three or four years those same kids in high school were listening to it."

ABOVE: Black Sabbath: A key musical influence for Nirvana and many Seattle "grunge" bands.

RIGHT: Seattle's Mudhoney, who shared a record label with Nirvana (Sub Pop) and would frequently appear on the bill with them. Matt Lukin (front, left), was originally a member of The Melvins; Dan Peters (front, right), would briefly serve as Nirvana's drummer.

Novoselic also made the jump to punk, though in a more roundabout fashion. Seeing his unhappiness in Aberdeen, Novoselic was sent to live with relatives in Croatia for a year, where he was exposed to the sounds of British punk and new wave. His interest in music was further spurred when he returned to Aberdeen and his mother bought him a guitar. He'd previously learned to play accordion as a child, and now spent much of his time perfecting his skills on the guitar, taking lessons at Rosevear's from the same man who'd taught Cobain, Warren Mason.

Mutual friends brought Novoselic into the Melvins' circle, where he struck up a friendship with Cobain. Over time, the two began jamming together. Given the lack of places to play in Aberdeen – at that point, only The Melvins had developed enough of a reputation to get gigs out of town – friends tended to get together for jam sessions at each other's homes, forming ad hoc groups that, at most, might play a local party.

By 1985, Novoselic had graduated from high school, while Cobain had dropped out. At the end of the year, Cobain returned to his aunt's house in Seattle, intending to make a more serious recording. He'd formed a group called Fecal Matter with Dale Crover on bass and Greg Hokanson on drums, but recorded the demo at his aunt's only with Crover (who played both drums and bass, as well as providing backing vocals). Back in Aberdeen, he dubbed off copies on cassette, which he called 'Illiteracy Will Prevail', to pass out to his friends, drawing artwork for each J-card: a large pile of excrement below the band's name.

Fecal Matter broke up without playing a single show, and the tapes of the band Cobain passed out initially failed to stir much interest. Undaunted, Cobain continued to seek out any opportunity, however slim, to advance his nascent career, playing occasionally with a Melvins' spin-off group called the Stiff Woodies (Novoselic also performed with the group), and performing as the opening act at a Melvins show in Olympia, Washington's state capitol, reading poetry while Osborne and Crover played behind him.

In the fall of 1986, Cobain and Matt Lukin moved into a small house in Aberdeen together. Novoselic, who'd been intrigued by Cobain's Fecal Matter tape, was a frequent visitor, and as they continued to jam together, decided it was time to take things to the next level. Cobain stuck with guitar, Novoselic switched to bass, and the two approached Aaron Burckhard, a drummer they knew who'd also hung out with The Melvins, and asked if he'd like to play with them. Burckhard agreed, "So we rounded up some drums and started practicing," he recalls. The band that would eventually become Nirvana had got its start at last.

EARLY RECORDINGS

As soon as he learned some chords on the guitar, Cobain began writing his own songs. Not much is known of his first demo, called *Organized Confusion*, recorded in December 1982, at his aunt Mari's home in Seattle, as no tracks from the recording have ever surfaced. Cobain played an electric guitar and used wooden spoons on a suitcase for the drums; Mari recalled the music as "a lot of distortion on guitar, really heavy bass, and the clucky sound of the wooden spoons. And his voice, sounding like he was mumbling under a big fluffy comforter, with some passionate screams once in a while."

Over the next few years, Cobain recorded other demos with his friends. The songs, none of which have surfaced, were primitively recorded on a boombox, and included such numbers as 'Venereal Girl' (set to the tune of Madonna's 'Material Girl'), 'Diamond Dave,' about the father of a friend, and 'Ode to Beau,' described in *Heavier Than Heaven* as a country-western number about a classmate who killed himself.

Only one song has been officially released from the *Illiteracy Will Prevail* tape, recorded in December 1985 at aunt Mari's home; 'Spank Thru,' which appeared on the 2005 collection *Sliver: The Best of the Box*. It's a surprisingly jaunty number, with lyrics that poke fun at the conventional pop song, an early indication of the strain of humor that ran through Nirvana's work from the beginning. The tape also features an early version of 'Downer,' with a heavily distorted guitar and stream-of-consciousness lyrics.

Both numbers would be re-recorded just over two years later at Nirvana's first professional demo session, produced by Jack Endino in Seattle. All but one of the 10 songs recorded for the so-called *Dale Demo* have since been officially released, making it easy to trace Nirvana's development from this point. The songs show Cobain's skills as a songwriter and musician becoming more sophisticated, for while there are certainly moments of Melvins-esque proto-grunge, like the exceptionally heavy 'Paper Cuts', Nirvana's own sensibility can be heard emerging on other tracks. Amidst the blurry guitars, melodies are becoming more refined, with the minor key settings giving the music a wash of sadness. But humour (if of a dark nature) is also evident, on numbers like 'Floyd the Barber,' and in the title of 'Aero Zeppelin' (which itself goes through an impressive number of tempo changes). And then there's the pull of Cobain's voice. Listen to the opening of 'If You Must,' with Cobain singing in a high, almost lilting tone, then unexpectedly launching himself into a mighty roar, and you can hear what first stunned Sub Pop's Jonathan Poneman when Jack Endino slipped him a copy of the demo.

> ## " A lot of distortion on guitar, really heavy bass, and the clucky sound of the wooden spoons. "

Kurt Cobain's Aunt Mari on his first recording

RIGHT: Guitarist Jason Everman was credited on the *Bleach* cover though he didn't play on it. But his contribution was just as important; he paid for the recording costs.

OPPOSITE: Nirvana prepared for the *Bleach* sessions with nightly rehearsals held at Krist Novoselic's mother's beauty parlor.

"Floyd The Barber" and "Paper Cuts" were the first songs from the *Dale Demo* to be officially released, on *Bleach* in June 1989. "Mexican Seafood," a grunting number about disease, was next, appearing on the *Teriyaki Asthma Vol. 1* EP released by C/Z Records in November 1989 (and later on the *Teriyaki Asthma Vol. IV* album released in 1991). "Beeswax," a punishing number with a frantic vocal workout, was first released on the 1991 compilation *Kill Rock Stars*. Both tracks later appeared on *Incesticide*.

The very first Nirvana record was the "Love Buzz"/"Big Cheese" single, released in November 1988. It was an atypical choice from Nirvana's song roster, and the band wasn't entirely happy about recording a cover for their first single; the song was originally by Dutch band Shocking Blue, best known for their hit "Venus." But Nirvana certainly gave their version a distinctive treatment, awash with psychedelic swirlings, neatly matched by drummer Chad Channing's crisp work, and Cobain's drawling vocals, particularly on the chorus. It was also an indication that the band wasn't only interested in hard rock; "Love Buzz" was the first Nirvana number one could really call a pop song. "Big Cheese" had a harder edge, leavened by a strong dose of sarcasm.

The version of "Spank Thru" that appears on *Sub Pop 200* (released in December 1988) has a lighter touch, no doubt due to Channing's presence on drums, as opposed to the version on the *Dale Demo*. It also sounds brighter, being in a higher key, and Cobain's vocal is more confident. Coupled with the release of "Love Buzz," the two songs revealed that Nirvana certainly wasn't a band steeped in stereotypical grunge.

Another early group session came in the spring of 1989, when Nirvana recorded at Evergreen State College with second guitarist Jason Everman — the only time the band ever recorded as a four piece. First up was a very loose cover of "Do You Love Me" for a Kiss compilation, with Cobain and Novoselic providing increasingly goofy vocals. More interesting is an early version of "Dive" that clearly points the way to *Nevermind*; thick, melodic guitars, and a bracing Cobain vocal.

OPPOSITE: Nirvana's first single, "Love Buzz"/"Big Cheese" was released in a limited edition run of 1,000 copies, making it a highly valued collector's item.

RIGHT: Charles Peterson's first photo session with Nirvana. Charles' photos would appear on many future Nirvana records, posters, and promotional photos.

KURT COBAIN

"Kurt was a completely creative person – a true artist," is how Krist Novoselic described his band mate in his memoir *Of Grunge and Government: Let's Fix This Broken Democracy!* Certainly as Nirvana's lead singer, guitarist, and primary songwriter, Kurt Cobain was the dominant creative force of the band, and it was his drive and determination that ultimately took Nirvana to the top of the charts.

Kurt Donald Cobain was born on February 20, 1967. Despite his troubled upbringing, with extended periods of time when he had no fixed residence (ironically, something true both before and after Nirvana found success), he always found an outlet for his artistic expression. When Novoselic began hanging out with Cobain in their late teens, he was struck by how many disciplines Cobain's talents encompassed. If he wasn't playing music or writing songs, he might be sketching in a notebook, making clay sculptures, or painting. He even turned TV viewing into a creative exercise, compiling video collages culled from the hours he spent watching and taping television shows, montages Novoselic called "scathing testimonies of popular culture...surreal sociology."

It was an artistic versatility that ended up having an influence on every aspect of Nirvana, making Cobain more than just a talented musician and songwriter; he was also someone who sought to express himself in as many different venues as possible. Cobain designed some of the band's early posters, for example. "Hey kids!" says a spectral figure on a poster advertising a 1988 show. "Don't buy a gram this weekend, come see a revelation in progress. It will be a gosh darn HEALING EXPLOSION." The tongue-in-cheek humor in the dialogue is evident, though Cobain's accompanying illustration is disturbing; a ghoulish Virgin Mary with blacked-out eyes and water dripping profusely off her hands (the poster can be seen in Michael Azerrad's Nirvana biography *Come As You Are*). It's a prime example of what Novoselic called the "dark thread" he saw present in "most of Kurt's creativity."

Certainly this "dark thread" can be seen in the artwork of Cobain's that was used on Nirvana's records. The 'Lithium' single features a shot of ghostly-looking dolls from Cobain's collection, while the back cover has a picture of a skeleton lying on a bed of flowers. Cobain expanded on this latter idea for the back cover of *In Utero*, which depicted an array of human bones and fetuses scattered on a bed of lilies. The artwork was deemed so objectionable, two prominent American chain stores refused to carry the album until the back cover was altered (a section of the collage without any fetuses was instead blown up to fill the back cover); the title of 'Rape Me' was changed to 'Waif Me.'

But there was no censoring the fetal imagery used in the 'Heart-Shaped Box' video (in one sequence, fetuses are seen hanging from creepy, gnarled trees), to the surprise of the video's director, Anton Corbijn. "That's pretty heavy stuff, in most people's book," he says. Novoselic himself referred to the video as "spooky as all hell."

LEFT: Kurt, at age six, with mother Wendy, father Don, and sister Kim. Kurt later described his early childhood as "blissful times."

OPPOSITE LEFT: Kurt, age 19, following an arrest for trespassing and underage drinking; when it was learned he had an outstanding warrant for "malicious mischief" (due to a previous vandalism charge) he was briefly sent to jail.

OPPOSITE RIGHT: Kurt in performance in Amsterdam, on November 25, 1991. The show was taped for Dutch TV; songs from the show later appeared in *Live! Tonight! Sold Out!!*

> "Kurt was a completely creative person – a true artist."
>
> Krist Novoselic

Cobain explained that the video's look was inspired by his own dreams, thus offering an enticing peek into his subconscious.

And darkness ran through all of Nirvana's music. There was never an out-and-out "happy" Nirvana song; even in 'Lithium's opening lines, when Cobain sings about being happy that he's found his friends, he twists the situation by adding "they're in my head." While the band worked on musical ideas together, the lyrics to Nirvana's songs were all Cobain's. As a lyricist, Cobain tended to look beneath the surface of events, juxtaposing contradictory statements as a means of determining his own truth. Ironically, though Cobain's lyrics were rarely straightforward, they touched such an emotional chord with listeners it was often felt that he'd revealed more than he actually had. After his death, so much was he seen as the long-suffering artist, it was believed that in the last Nirvana song, 'You Know You're Right,' he howled the word "pain" during the chorus. Actually, as the isolated vocal track used on the game *Guitar Hero* shows, he was simply singing "hey."

Cobain's contradictory nature added to his appeal. Though described during his life as a reluctant star, it was later learned that he complained to his managers if he felt that Nirvana's videos weren't being screened enough on TV. Cobain's early death made him a legend, and, to some, the fact that he'd killed himself made him a martyr. Though acknowledging what he calls the "deity" aspect of Cobain's story, Novoselic downplays it: "That's for people who need the mystique." And while having a mystique is something that differentiates between the good and the great, it's true it shouldn't be allowed to overshadow Cobain's true accomplishments: he was an artist with a unique vision, who was able to turn his personal concerns into works of art that resonated with audiences around the world.

OPPOSITE LEFT: Kurt at the 1993 MTV Video Music awards with wife Courtney Love and daughter Frances Bean Cobain.

OPPOSITE RIGHT: One of Kurt's famous battered guitars.

RIGHT: Kurt in London, October 1990. Kurt's off-the-wall sensibility gave Nirvana's work a touch of unpredictability.

1987 TO BLEACH

As 1986 turned into 1987, Cobain's Aberdeen home became the focal point for the as-yet-unnamed group. "We had the most intense jams," Novoselic recalled. "We'd simultaneously orbit inner and outer space. It was so serious, if we felt we sucked at rehearsal we were disappointed and we'd sit around bummed out after." Burckhard was already less enamored than the other two about putting so much effort into what was for him more of a hobby. "It was practice non-stop," he says. "It was like practice, practice, practice, all the time. It kind of got to me, you know. I just wasn't into practicing a lot." It was an early sign of a rift that would only grow bigger.

LEFT: Legendary producer Jack Endino produced half of Nirvana's recording sessions, including their very first professional demo session on January 23, 1988.

OPPOSITE: Kurt, Chad, and Krist during their first show of 1989, at Portland, Oregon's Satyricon Club, when they shared the bill with Mudhoney.

The band made their public debut in March 1987 at a party in Raymond, another small town in the area. The date had been arranged by Ryan Aigner, a fellow Aberdonian who knew the two men who lived in the Raymond house, Jeff Franks and Tony Poukkula. Both were musicians, and Burckhard was relieved he'd be able to play Franks' Tama drum set and thus not have to bring his own kit. Surprisingly, the show was also documented; Franks snapped a picture of a group, and an audio recording was also made, since widely bootlegged.

Though the show has sometimes been described as a near disaster (Novoselic has denied that anything truly outrageous occurred), the recording reveals a pretty straightforward performance. Out of the nine songs played, all were originals, save for a medley of Led Zeppelin's 'Heartbreaker' that segued into 'How Many More Times,' performed after Novoselic played the song's opening riff, the party goers then shouting at the band to continue. Though the original songs had a metal influence, they also had an edgier feel, due to Cobain's and Novoselic's interest in punk and new wave acts (Burckhard described himself as more of a "metal head"). The mixing of musical genres that would be a key reason for Nirvana's crossover appeal was present from their very first show.

RIGHT: Mudhoney's Mark Arm on the same night. The two bands frequently toured together.

"It was like practice, practice, practice, all the time. It kind of got to me, you know. I just wasn't into practicing a lot."

Aaron Burckhard

LEFT and OPPOSITE: From photographer Alice Wheeler's session for the "Love Buzz" single.

Cobain later claimed the show was an extravagant noise fest featuring the band playing Flipper's 'Sex Bomb' for an hour (a song they didn't actually play), delighting in "freaking out" the "redneck" audience. The reality was a bit more prosaic, though Cobain's girlfriend, Tracy Marander, admitted they were acting "goofy, because everyone seemed like they were uptight." In this instance, "goofiness" involved running around the living room, with Novoselic leaping off the TV cabinet and occasionally out the window. "Everyone's like, 'You're going to break stuff!'" Marandar recalled. Aigner conceded, "It was obvious they did not fit in with the people there … Everyone else from Raymond was like, 'What is this freak show?'" but the band was able to play for nearly an hour, and even received some positive comments on leaving for home.

The band played sporadically over the next year, under various names, including Skid Row, Bliss, Pen Cap Chew (also the name of one of their songs), and Ted Ed Fred, mostly in Olympia and Tacoma (a city roughly midway between Olympia and Seattle). Novoselic and his girlfriend soon moved to Tacoma, where he worked as an industrial painter; Cobain and his girlfriend moved to Olympia, where he occasionally worked as a janitor. Burckhard remained in Aberdeen, and when Cobain and Novoselic decided they wanted to record a professional demo, they went looking for a new drummer.

When no one suitable could be located, Dale Crover was asked to fill in. This proved to be helpful when Cobain called Reciprocal Recording in Seattle to book a session. It was producer Jack Endino who answered the phone, and, on hearing that the trio of musicians included Crover, agreed to work with them himself, being well aware of Crover's growing reputation as a formidable drummer.

And so, on January 23, 1988, Cobain, Novoselic, and Crover arrived in Seattle. The group worked quickly, recording 10 songs in six hours (for a total cost of $152.44), before leaving for a show that evening in Tacoma. The songs were again all originals (Novoselic noted that Cobain had little interest in playing covers), and emphasized the powerful nature of the band's music, greatly aided in this instance by having Crover on drums.

Endino was impressed enough to ask the band if he could make a copy of what was eventually called the "Dale Demo" for himself. It was a request that would end up immediately boosting the band's profile, for Endino passed out copies to various well-chosen friends: one copy was given to a DJ at the University of Washington's college radio station, KCMU, resulting in the band's first airplay; one was given to Endino's girlfriend, Dawn Anderson, who wrote the first article about the band; and another was given to Jonathan Poneman at Sub Pop Records, who would release the band's first records.

"We had the most intense jams. We'd simultaneously orbit inner and outer space. It was so serious."

Krist Novoselic

The band was as yet unaware of these developments. The Melvins were relocating to San Francisco, meaning Crover was due to leave; he recommended another Aberdonian, Dave Foster, as his replacement. Foster did have the distinction of playing the band's first show in Seattle, but his tenure was brief, when he lost his driver's license as the result of being in a fight, and could no longer attend practices. Aaron Burckhard then returned to the lineup, but fell out of favor when he was arrested for drunk driving while behind the wheel of Cobain's car. Cobain and Novoselic then approached another drummer they'd seen while playing shows, Chad Channing, and asked if he'd like to jam with them. Channing agreed, not understanding the low-key request was actually an offer to join the band. After a few rehearsals, he realized Cobain and Novoselic considered him a full-fledged member.

By then, Cobain had settled on a name for the group: Nirvana, which first appeared on a poster for a March 19, 1988 show at Tacoma's Community World Theater. He later explained he wanted a mellow name instead of a "mean, raunchy punk name" – though mean, raunchy punk was a fair assessment of what the band was actually playing.

But Nirvana always had a strong pop element bubbling up under the surface, as became apparent when they recorded their first single. Jonathan Poneman had been excited about the band since hearing the "Dale Demo", though his business partner at Sub Pop, Bruce Pavitt, was more uncertain. But after seeing the band a few times in Seattle, he agreed to release a single, and Nirvana returned to Reciprocal in June, recording five songs in two sessions, along with early versions of three songs that would later appear on *Bleach*.

A cover of Shocking Blue's 'Love Buzz' was the designated A-side, with an original number, 'Big Cheese,' inspired by Poneman, on the B-side. Final overdubs and mixing were done in July; Cobain had crafted a 30 second sound collage, drawn from his record and tape collection, that he wanted to tack on to the beginning of 'Love Buzz,' but Pavitt and Poneman insisted it be cut down to 10 seconds. The cover featured the first of many deliberate misspellings of Cobain's name: he was credited as "Kurdt Kobain."

The band was pleased to have completed their first single, which was released that November, the first release in Sub Pop's "Singles Club," where subscribers received limited edition singles. Hot on its heels came Nirvana's second release, on *Sub Pop 200*, a compilation of three EPs featuring various up-and-coming Seattle acts, including Soundgarden, Mudhoney, and Tad in addition to Nirvana. Nirvana's contribution to the set was a re-recording of 'Spank Thru' (which had appeared on the "Dale Demo"), recorded during the 'Love Buzz' session and featuring backing vocals from Jack Endino.

Nirvana celebrated the end of the year by going back into the studio to record their first album, recording nine songs over six sessions in December 1988 and January 1989. The band was well rehearsed – "They just banged it out," Endino recalled – though everyone would occasionally have to wait for Cobain to finish the lyrics. In contrast with the songs on the "Dale Demo", the new songs were more direct, and, in some cases, lyrically stripped to the bone ('School' only has 15 words). Alienation, dysfunction, and depression are the dominant themes; even 'About A Girl,' a standout track quickly noted for its pretty, Beatles-esque melody, had lyrics that offered a sardonic critique of Cobain's relationship with his girlfriend. The album was rounded out with the band's last single and two tracks from the *Dale Demo*.

In January 1989, Nirvana officially signed with Sub Pop Records. There were four signatures on the contract; the band had enlisted Jason Everman, a friend of Channing's, as a second guitarist, helping to fill out their sound. Nirvana also began playing further afield, first in the neighboring state of Oregon, then down to California. While in San Francisco, Cobain was taken with signs advising IV drug users to 'Bleach Your Works,' to help curtail the spread of the AIDS virus, and decided Nirvana's new album would be called *Bleach*.

That spring, Everman played his only session with Nirvana. Using a studio at the Evergreen State College in Olympia, the band recorded a cover of Kiss' 'Do You Love Me' for a Kiss compilation, along with an early version of the song 'Dive.' *Bleach* was ready for release in June. Then it was time for Nirvana to head out on the road on their first U.S. tour.

LEFT: More outtakes from the "Love Buzz" photo session. The shots were taken at Never Never Land, a public park in Tacoma, the city where Krist was living at the time.

BLEACH

If Nirvana had not gone on to achieve the enormous success they did, would *Bleach* be much remembered? Probably not, though it undoubtedly would have achieved a kind of cult status, touted as an example of potential unfulfilled. But as it happened, that potential was gloriously fulfilled, and thus *Bleach* is now seen as one in a series of stepping stones that led Nirvana to scale unimagined heights.

A heavy air of claustrophobia hangs over *Bleach*, especially on the tracks that originally bookended the album: 'Blew' and 'Sifting.' The former touches on what would be a familiar theme in Nirvana's songs: the oppressive nature of relationships, sung over the kind of mesmerizing drone also common to Nirvana's songs. 'Sifting' is a good deal heavier, its opening thudding beats setting an ominous mood, with lyrics that hit against typical authority figures (teachers and preachers). At over five minutes, it's the album's longest track, and does rather exemplify what Cobain later dismissively referred to as *Bleach*'s "one dimensional" quality. He was soon writing better, stronger material, though while 'Sifting' disappeared from the band's set lists after 1990, they played 'Blew' right up to their very last show, on March 1, 1994.

Bleach's sludgier tracks reveal the Melvins' influence, and they're also the least interesting. 'Paper Cuts' does at least benefit from having powerful drumming of The Melvins' Dale Crover (who also drums on 'Downer' and 'Floyd The Barber,' all three tracks taken from the band's first professional demo recorded with Jack Endino), and even refers to the band's name, here pronounced "Nir-van-uh" instead of "Nir-vah-nuh." But the song repeatedly circles back in on itself without going anywhere. 'Scoff' is an up-tempo rant about one's perceived inadequacy (a theme Cobain would explore in future songs like 'Stain' and 'Even In His Youth'), though there's a defiant giddiness in the chorus, with its whining demand for alcohol.

Both 'Swap Meet' and 'Mr. Moustache' are pen portraits about the kind of characters Cobain was trying to distance himself from: the "rednecks" that populated the area where he grew up. It was a stereotype he was unhappy being associated with, telling one interviewer, "I feel like we've been tagged as illiterate redneck cousin-fucking kids that have no idea what's going on at all. That's completely untrue."

'Swap Meet,' set to a propulsive beat, concerns a couple who make their living selling detritus at the local sales of the title, while stuck in a relationship whose main component is a severe lack of communication. 'Mr. Moustache' ups the tempo further in its depiction of a man mired in ignorance. Yet Cobain retains a degree of empathy for his subjects. Neither song is mean-spirited, and even Mr. Moustache himself isn't totally clueless, sarcastically commenting on those who see themselves as superior to him.

And when Cobain turns the focus to himself, he delights in self-deprecation. In 'Negative Creep's four lines, he neatly juxtaposes the band's own failings (with the opening statement about the song being "out of our range") and his own inherent pessimism with unabashed glee. 'School' pulls off the same trick, but even more concisely; in a mere 15 words, Cobain attacks stultifying conformity, but with such relish it sounds deliriously celebratory (his shrieks of "No recess!" are especially captivating).

The album's stand out tracks couldn't be more different musically. The sinister 'Floyd The Barber' takes the characters from the sitcom *The Andy Griffith Show* and has them torturing and assaulting the luckless narrator who wanders into Floyd

ABOVE: The 1992 Australian Tour Edition of *Bleach* is one of the rarest pressings of Nirvana's first album.

RIGHT: Kurt in performance, shortly after the Bleach sessions were completed.

> **"I feel like we've been tagged as illiterate redneck cousin-f***ing kids that have no idea what's going on at all. That's completely untrue."**
>
> Kurt Cobain

Lawson's barber shop for a shave, with Crover's intense pounding heightening the tension. As if sensing that a break might be needed after such a nightmare, 'Floyd' is followed by 'About A Girl,' whose melancholy tune helps disguise the fact that this supposed love song (written about Cobain's girlfriend) has a surprisingly petulant lyric. Unlike 'Love Buzz,' with its squalling guitars, 'About A Girl' was out-and-out sweet pop.

Bleach was given a slightly different character in the US and UK on its first release (June 1989 in the US, August 1989 in the UK). In the US, 'Love Buzz' appeared on the album, emphasizing the band's pop quotient; in the UK, the single's flip side, 'Big Cheese,' was used in its place (in both cases, the song followed 'School.' The CD featured both tracks, and added 'Downer,' which in this version (it dates back to the 1985 Fecal Matter tape) races along so briskly it comes in at under two minutes. It's also atypically wordy for a Nirvana song (the stripped-down 'School' offers a better indication of where Cobain was heading lyrically). The 2009 CD edition of the album has superior sound and a bonus disc featuring Nirvana's February 9, 1990 gig at the Pine Street Theatre in Portland, Oregon.

Cobain was right to find *Bleach* a flawed album, but it's hardly one-dimensional. All the elements that would enable Nirvana to crossover to the mainstream – strong hooks, the rock/pop/punk mix, Cobain's always compelling vocals – are present. Over the next two years, these elements would be constantly refined, finally coming together in a spectacular, and irresistible, combination.

OPPOSITE: A winsome portrait from the 'Love Buzz' photo session.

RIGHT: Nirvana's first visit to New York City, July 1989. Just days later, Jason Everman (left) would leave the band.

BLEACH TOUR TO GROHL'S ARRIVAL

The same month *Bleach* was released, Nirvana played their biggest show to date, Sub Pop's first "Lame Fest," at Seattle's Moore Theatre on June 9. The band was third on the bill, opening for Tad and Mudhoney, and received an enthusiastic write up from *Backlash*, a local rock magazine, who noted approvingly that Nirvana's set was "totally intense." The magazine's editor, Dawn Anderson, had written the very first article about Nirvana, published the previous August in Backlash, in which she'd said, "At the risk of sounding blasphemous, I honestly believe that with enough practice, Nirvana could become . . . better than the Melvins!"

Now the band headed out on their first US tour, playing 21 shows in just under a month. There was little money, never more than $100 a night, and with food and gas the main priorities, the band sometimes found themselves sleeping by the side of the road. New band t-shirts brought in some extra income. On the front was the band's name and a picture of the circles of hell from Dante's *Inferno* Cobain had seen in a book, while on the back was a phrase Novoselic had come up with: "Fudge Packin', Crack Smokin', Satan Worshippin' Motherfuckers."

As would become a pattern on every subsequent long Nirvana tour, Cobain began feeling increasingly unwell (due to a long-standing stomach condition that was never properly diagnosed, and a marked propensity to catch colds). Nor was Jason Everman working out as well as everyone hoped. Cobain and Novoselic felt he had more a "rock" sensibility as opposed to a punk aesthetic, while Everman was unhappy at having so little say in the group's musical direction; "I always felt kind of peripheral," he later said. By the time Nirvana reached New York City in July, communication between Everman and the other band members had largely broken down. Cobain told Novoselic privately that he'd decided to kick Everman out of the band, then announced to all that the tour was over. The drive home across the country was completed in silence.

In August, Cobain and Novoselic teamed up with Mark Lanegan and Mark Pickerel, two members of another Seattle act, Screaming Trees, to form a blues band side project. "What we were trying to do was a modern-day version of Cream or Led Zeppelin," Pickerel explains, envisioning a group that might cover everyone from Robert Johnson to Johnny Cash. Cobain and Lanegan were fans of Huddie "Leadbelly" Ledbetter in particular, so during their ad hoc group's two recording sessions (produced by Jack Endino) they focused on his work, recording covers of 'Where Did You Sleep Last Night,' 'Ain't It A Shame,' 'They Hung Him On A Cross,' and 'Grey Goose.' It was a rare instance of the two bands recording cover songs, and Cobain's vocal on 'Ain't It A Shame' was especially riveting, but the musicians, who jokingly dubbed themselves The Jury, never reconvened again. 'Where Did You Sleep Last Night' soon appeared on Lanegan's solo LP, *The Winding Sheet*, while the other three tracks wouldn't be released until 2004, on Nirvana's box set *With The Lights Out*.

The following month, Nirvana, now back to a three piece, entered the studio to record some tracks for an upcoming EP, *Blew*, which would feature two songs from *Bleach*, and two new songs. The session, held at Seattle's Music Source studio and produced by Steve Fisk, saw the group firmly headed in a more pop direction. "The songs were a little more pop, a little more along the lines of 'About a Girl,'" Channing agrees. "So they felt really comfortable." 'Been A Son' and 'Stain' (which ended up on the EP) wedded brisk, upbeat melodies to dark-themed lyrics, as did an early version of 'Even In His Youth.' It was also the first time the group recorded the even darker 'Polly,' a disturbing portrait of violence from the perpetrator's perspective. The band also recorded a song that would never be completed, the droning, rhythmic 'Token Eastern Song.'

In late September the group headed out on a short US tour to make up for the dates they'd cancelled when they'd shortened their summer US tour. They then began their first European tour in late October, which took 36 days, the first date on what was named the "Heavier Than Heaven" tour being October 23 at the Riverside in Newcastle. Also on the tour was fellow Sub Pop act Tad (the two bands alternating as headliners), with both acts and their two-man crew traveling in one packed van.

While in England, Nirvana recorded a session for BBC Radio 1's John Peel Show on October 26, performing 'Love Buzz,' 'About A Girl,' 'Polly,' and 'Spank Thru' (broadcast on November 22). In the Netherlands, they recorded a live session for VPRO Radio's Nozems-a-Gogo program, performing 'Love Buzz,' 'Dive,' and 'About A Girl.' Interestingly, though the music press was covering the band as a heavy power trio, the band chose to emphasize their pop leanings in their radio sessions.

After the Netherlands, the tour moved on to West Germany, Austria, Hungary, and Italy. Thanks to coverage in the British music weeklies (of which there were four at the time) and other local

RIGHT: Kurt at the Sub Pop Lame Fest held in London, at the end of the band's first European tour.

BELOW: A ticket from Nirvana's debut performance in London, October 27, 1989, at the University of London's School of Oriental and African Studies.

OPPOSITE ABOVE LEFT: Nirvana's *Bleach*-era t-shirts featured a depiction of the circles of hell from Dante's *Inferno* that Kurt found in a book at the Aberdeen Public Library.

coverage, Sub Pop bands enjoyed a cult-like reputation in England and Europe, and the shows were well attended. The band also made the front cover of a magazine for the first time, in the October 21 issue of UK weekly *Sounds* (though Nirvana was relegated to a small box while Tad assumed most of the cover space). But with so little time off, the stress of touring soon caught up with the musicians, especially Cobain, who was again ill, having told Tad's Kurt Danielson "I've wanted to go home since the first week of the tour." At a show in Rome on November 27, Cobain's fragile psyche cracked publicly, as sound problems during Nirvana's set led him to climb a speaker stack and threaten to jump. The bouncers managed to get him down, but he was still highly distressed backstage. "It was the first time I heard him say, 'I see all these people in the crowd and they're fucking idiots,'" recalled Jonathan Poneman, who had flown over with Bruce Pavitt to catch the end of the tour.

Cobain also announced he wanted to quit the band and go home, but Poneman calmed him down and traveled with him via train to Switzerland the next day. Unfortunately, Cobain's wallet and passport were stolen while he was asleep on the train, but Poneman worked the situation out with the authorities and the tour continued, with further shows in Belgium and France. The tour's final night was at London's Astoria on December 3, Sub Pop's second "Lame Fest," with Sub Pop band Mudhoney added to the bill. Though Nirvana didn't rate their set very highly ("It stunk," Novoselic recalled), two songs from the set would appear on the posthumously released live album *From The Muddy Banks of the Wishkah*. The band ended their set with a flourish, Novoselic wielding his bass like a baseball bat and smashing Cobain's guitar.

The band arrived home to find themselves on the cover of the December issue of Seattle music paper *The Rocket* — their first full cover. Cobain recorded a guest appearance on Lanegan's *The Winding Sheet* (backing vocals on 'Down In the Dark'), his second such appearance that year — he'd previously played guitar on a single by Olympia band The Go Team. On New Year's Eve, Novoselic married his girlfriend Shelli. Two days later, Nirvana was back in the studio, working on a single song, 'Sappy,' with Jack Endino at Reciprocal, over two sessions. It was in the vein of the

RIGHT: Kurt makes his London debut on October 27, 1989. Kurt ended the raucous show by setting off a fire extinguisher.

BELOW: Kurt Cobain and Nirvana performing live at the School of Oriental and African Studies in London in 1989.

"I've wanted to go home since the first week of the tour."

Kurt Cobain

poppier songs the band had been doing more of, but they would never end up recording a satisfactory version of it. Endino was puzzled as to why they spend so much time on the song; "It just didn't seem that interesting," he says.

There was a short West Coast tour in February. Before the band headed out on the road again, they shot some videos at Evergreen, intending to use the footage on a video they could sell at their shows. Three of the songs were from the *Bleach* era; 'School,' 'Big Cheese,' and 'Floyd The Barber.' There was also a new song, 'Lithium,' which the band had yet to play live; boasting a solid pop hook and a crunchy chorus designed for fist-pumping, it thrilled the film crew, all Nirvana fans. The videos were never officially released, but have been widely bootlegged; an interesting element is that the backing footage used on 'School' was drawn from Cobain's collection of random material videotaped from TV; 'Floyd' featured home movie footage of his toy collection.

In April, the band began another US tour, which again took them across the country to the East Coast. But there was also another purpose to the tour, with the band taking five days off to record what was set to be their next album for Sub Pop, at Smart Studios in Madison, Wisconsin, with Butch Vig producing. The band recorded eight songs. Four had been a part of the band's set for some time ('Immodium,' later renamed 'Breed,' 'Polly,' 'Dive,' and 'Sappy'), three were new ('In Bloom,' 'Lithium,' and 'Pay To Play,' later renamed 'Stay Away'), and one was a cover, 'Here She Comes Now,' destined for a Velvet Underground compilation. The sessions went fairly smoothly, though Vig noticed some tension between Cobain and Channing over the latter's drumming.

After the sessions were done, the tour continued through May 17. There was little of the drama of other tours, and audiences were bigger. "Some of the most fun places to play were in the Midwest," Channing told author Greg Prato. "I think its just because they didn't get a whole lot of bands coming through there." While in New York City, Nirvana shot a more professional video for the just recorded 'In Bloom.' With most of their second album completed, Nirvana seemed poised to step up to even more popularity. But a sudden change would keep them in a holding pattern for more than a year.

OPPOSITE and RIGHT: More shots of Nirvana during Jason Everman's tenure in 1989. Nirvana wouldn't take on another fourth member until 1993, when Pat Smear joined as second guitarist.

the skulsuk club

SUNDAY 1ST OCTOBER   FROM USA

DAS DAMEN £3.50/£3
+WALKING SEEDS   + dr. phibes

SUNDAY 8TH OCTOBER

from australia hard-ons

+ BOMB DISNEYLAND   + IDENTITY
ADVANCE TICKETS £3.50

SUNDAY 15TH OCTOBER   *from USA*

bitch magnet £3.50/£3
+ THE CATERAN   + slum turkeys

SUNDAY 22ND OCTOBER

junior manson slags
+ SCREAMING MARIONETTES
+ SUPPORT   £3/£2.50

SUNDAY 29TH OCTOBER   SUB POP '89   FROM SEATTLE

TAD + NIRVANA
+ SUPPORT   ADVANCE TICKET £3.50

advance tickets: VINYL DREAMS + FRANKS
edwards no.8, sunday nights 7.30▸10.30

ABOVE: Flyer advertising Nirvana's appearance in Birmingham,
their fifth UK concert in 1989.

RIGHT: A flyer from one of the band's first UK concerts, sharing
the bill with Tad.

OPPOSITE: Nirvana in a jovial mood on Seattle's waterfront,
circa 1989. Note Jason's Soundgarden t-shirt; he would join
Soundgarden after leaving Nirvana.

LET THERE BE ROCK!

PHOTO: CHARLES PETERSON

T A D / N I R V A N A
SUB POP GLITTER/SWEAT-FEST

Oct. 23-30	United Kingdom
Nov. 1- 5	Netherlands
Nov. 8	Cologne, Rose Club
Nov. 9	Hannover, Bad
Nov. 10	Enger, Forum
Nov. 11	Berlin, Ecstasy
Nov. 12	Oldenburg, Alhambra
Nov. 13	Hamburg, Fabrik
Nov. 15	To Be Announced
Nov. 16	Nürnberg, Trust
Nov. 17	Gammelsdorf, Circus
Nov. 18	Hanua, Kuba
Nov. 20-26	Austria
Nov. 28- Dec. 4	Switzerland
Dec. 4-10	Italy

Glitterhouse
RECORDS
LANGE STR. 41 · 3471 LAUENFÖRDE
WEST GERMANY

Ph.: 05273-7831
Fax: 05273-8505

DAVE GROHL

When Dave Grohl joined Nirvana, the last piece of the puzzle finally fell into place for the band. For it was Grohl's drumming that transformed Nirvana from a good band into a veritable powerhouse.

David Eric Grohl was born on January 14, 1969 in Warren, Ohio, but grew up primarily in Springfield, Virginia, a suburb of Washington, D.C., where he remained with his mother and sister after his parents divorced when he was seven. The first instrument Grohl picked up was the trombone, but his interest in rock music meant that it wasn't too long before he picked up a guitar. He played that instrument in his first band, Freak Baby, but by the time Freak Baby changed their name to Mission Impossible he'd moved to the drum kit.

It is that musical versatility that's led to Grohl being an especially hard working musician. Even when he was in Nirvana, he continued working on his own music on the side, in addition to other side projects. A number of the songs Grohl wrote during his early time with Nirvana ended up on the 1992 *Pocketwatch* cassette (not released under his own name; instead, he was credited as a mysterious artist named "Late"), and others surfaced on the debut Foo Fighters album. He also played drums on Buzz Osborne's solo album, 1992's *King Buzzo* (credited as "Dale Nixon"), and performed in the all-star, alt-rock band put together to provide the music for the Beatles' bio-pic *Backbeat*, released in 1994.

Oddly, Nirvana never drew on Grohl's songwriting skills; his only contribution would be the song 'Marigold,' which appeared as a B-side on the 'Heart-Shaped Box' single. Not that he was then relegated to "only" being the band's drummer; Grohl played drums with sufficient force that his beats become as melodic as they are rhythmic. Grohl also provided harmonizing vocals, which brought a new color to the band, as you can hear on the choruses of 'In Bloom' and 'Polly.' It's the opening guitar riff of 'Smells Like Teen Spirit' that makes it so instantly recognizable, but there would surely be something missing from the song if Grohl hadn't also been behind the drum kit. His reputation as a hard-hitter made tracks like 'Scentless Apprentice' and 'Radio Friendly Unit Shifter' absolute standouts, but he was capable of playing with a lighter touch as well, as evidenced by his work on the Unplugged show.

Grohl joined Nirvana as the band was about to take off; a year and four months after he joined, Nirvana was topping the Billboard charts, and three years and three months later, Kurt Cobain was dead. It made the experience an exceptionally wild ride for Grohl, and he dealt with the aftermath by going back to work, recording the Foo Fighters album in little more than a week in the fall of 1994, playing all the instruments himself, save for a guitar part on 'X-Static,' played by Greg Dulli of Afghan Whigs. It was the opening chapter of the next phase of his life, which would see him steering Foo Fighters to becoming one of rock's top acts, with eight studio albums and numerous Grammys to their credit – so far.

OPPOSITE: Dave Grohl's joining Nirvana turned the band into "a force of nature," as Krist Novoselic put it.

RIGHT: Dave in London, October 1990, a month after he became Nirvana's drummer.

" His contribution transformed us into a force of nature."

Krist Novoselic on Dave Grohl

Being in one groundbreaking band and following that up by founding another successful group would be enough for most people. Not Grohl. His side project band Probot (who released a single, self-titled album in 2004) allowed him to work with his metal/hard rock heroes like King Diamond and Lemmy. He recorded and toured with Queens of the Stone Age, and in 2009, he formed another power trio, Them Crooked Vultures, with Queens' Josh Homme and Led Zeppelin's John Paul Jones. In part, these excursions gave Grohl a chance to play drums again, as he's a guitarist in the Foos. But it's clear the main incentive is that he simply likes to play music as much as possible with whoever is willing. A look at the number of records he's made guest appearances on proves that; it's a list than encompasses David Bowie, Mike Watt, The Bangles, Nine Inch Nails, Killing Joke, and Puff Daddy, to name a few.

Through it all, Grohl has remained remarkably grounded; not prone to putting on rock star airs, he's often described as "the nicest man in rock." Though his first marriage ended in divorce, his second marriage, to former MTV producer Jordyn Blum, has been more successful; married in 2003, the couple now has two daughters. He remains especially close to his mother, buying a house for her in LA near his own home. He's equally at home with old friends from his past and the new friends his profession has allowed him to meet – like Paul McCartney, a friendship that led to Grohl accompanying Sir Paul to the White House in 2010, when McCartney was given the Library of Congress Gershwin Prize for Popular Song by President Barack Obama. It's quite a journey, from the hardcore clubs of D.C. to the center of political power in the Free World. But it's a trip the good-natured Grohl has managed to take in his stride.

BELOW: A shot that jokingly establishes Dave as the boss of his highly successful post-Nirvana band, Foo Fighters.

ABOVE: In 2009, Dave joined Them Crooked Vultures, which also featured Led Zeppelin's John Paul Jones and Queens of the Stone Age's Josh Homme.

OPPOSITE: Though a multi-instrumentalist, Dave Grohl's power as a drummer is especially formidable.

G 40

GROHL TO *NEVERMIND*

With Nirvana's fortunes seemingly on the upswing, it was a strange time for the band to make a major change in the lineup. But after Nirvana's spring tour, Cobain and Novoselic showed up unexpectedly at Chad Channing's home and told him he was out of the band. Cobain had been increasingly unhappy with Channing's drumming, which wasn't as powerful as he wanted. For his part, Channing was unhappy he wasn't more involved in the songwriting, Cobain having previously suggested he might welcome some help but never following up on the offer. "I just started losing my inspiration to play," Channing told Greg Prato. "It shows. Ultimately, I didn't give them much choice but to kick me out of the band."

BELOW: Kurt crowd surfing at the Motor Sports International Garage show, the largest gig Nirvana had played in Seattle at that point.

Without a drummer, the band couldn't do any shows. But Nirvana was increasingly becoming a hot property, as was the budding alternative rock scene. Sub Pop had been seeking a partnership with a major label themselves, but Cobain and Novoselic felt it would be better to sign to a major directly. Susan Silver, then Soundgarden's manager, invited them to come to LA when she was there on business, and introduced them to music lawyer Alan Mintz, who agreed to help them look for a deal. The songs they'd recorded at Smart were no longer considered for a second Sub Pop album; they were instead shopped as demos to other labels.

Cobain and Novoselic then learned that Mudhoney drummer Dan Peters was looking for a new gig, Mudhoney being on a momentary break, and quickly contacted him; thus Peters found himself behind the kit when Nirvana next entered Reciprocal on July 11 to record a new single. Sub Pop, perhaps sensing that Nirvana was about to leave the label, wanted the recording done in a hurry, so 'Sliver' was laid down in one hour during a break in a Tad session (overdubs and vocals were completed on July 24). The song distilled a seemingly mundane incident from childhood – the narrator spending the night with his grandparents – into

two-and-a-half minutes of pure pop, an unexpectedly sweet song in the Nirvana catalogue, despite the roaring guitars that swoop in during the chorus.

Cobain and Novoselic had already arranged for Dale Crover to fill in on drums during a short tour that began in Las Vegas, then went through California, Oregon, and Washington before ending in Vancouver, British Columbia. Nirvana opened for one of their idols, Sonic Youth. Sonic Youth were also admirers of Nirvana, talking up the band to their management company, Gold Mountain, who would take on Nirvana as a client in a few months.

LEFT: Kurt wearing a Leadbelly shirt. Kurt was a big admirer of the blues/folk musician, whose version of 'Where Did You Sleep Last Night?' would prompt Nirvana to cover the song.

ABOVE LEFT: Kurt sometimes wore dresses, stating he found them comfortable. The entire band would wear dresses in Nirvana's 1992 video 'In Bloom.'

ABOVE RIGHT: April 1990: With bass and beer in hand, Krist prepares for yet another show.

When the tour hit San Francisco, Cobain and Novoselic had gone to see Washington, D.C. based hardcore band Scream play at the I-Beam, later commenting to Buzz Osborne how great they thought the drummer was (they'd also seen the band play a few weeks earlier in Olympia). The drummer was Dave Grohl, a versatile musician from the Washington, D.C. area. Musically, he'd followed the same pop-hard rock-punk rock trajectory Cobain and Novoselic had, and Scream was his third band.

But Cobain and Novoselic had seen the band when it was on its last legs; Scream was on a final US tour that fell apart soon after the San Francisco show, leaving Grohl at loose ends in LA. He phoned Osborne, whom he'd known for some years, and told him of his predicament. Osborne suggested he phone Nirvana, which he did, only to be told the group had engaged Peters as their new drummer. But only hours later, Novoselic phoned back and invited Grohl up to Washington to audition.

Perhaps Cobain and Novoselic were feeling some buyer's remorse. On September 22, they played a big show in Seattle with Peters on drums that was well received, and next day all three musicians posed for photos for a Nirvana piece in the UK weekly *Sounds*. But what Peters didn't know was that Grohl, who was then staying at Novoselic's house in Tacoma, had also been rehearsing with Nirvana, and they'd decided to make him their drummer. The news was first announced publicly on September 25, when Cobain

ABOVE: Three years after the band was formed, Nirvana finally had the classic line-up that would conquer the world: Dave Grohl, Kurt Cobain and Krist Novoselic.

RIGHT: Calm Before The Storm: Nirvana in Piccadilly Circus, London, shortly before the release of *Nevermind*.

made a surprise appearance on KAOS radio, after which Peters was finally informed of the change. He was disappointed, but soon found new work, briefly drumming with Screaming Tree, then joining Mudhoney again when they reformed.

Grohl played his first show with the band the following month on October 11 at Olympia's North Shore Surf Club. Though the set was initially plagued with sound problems, the band regained enough steam to turn in a solid performance, Grohl playing so ferociously he destroyed his snare, which Cobain proudly held up to display to the audience afterwards. A huge admirer of the Melvins, Grohl was a heavy hitter in the fashion of Dale Crover; indeed, Cobain had described him as "a baby Dale Crover." It was just the kind of invigorating power Nirvana's music had needed.

Less than two weeks later, Nirvana was back in the UK for a quick six-date tour. On October 21, they taped another John Peel session (broadcast on November 3), and unusually all the songs were covers: 'Son of a Gun' and 'Molly's Lips' by the Vaselines (an

act that was a particular favorite of Cobain's), 'D-7' by the Wipers, and Devo's 'Turnaround.'

After returning to the States, Grohl moved in with Cobain in Olympia. The next show the band played, on November 25 at Seattle's Off Ramp club, was one of the most important in their career, attended by several A&R reps all anxious to sign them. Nirvana eventually chose to sign with DGC, a subsidiary of Geffen Records that was also home to Sonic Youth – a key reason the band ended up on the label.

The deal wouldn't be finalized until April, but Gold Mountain put the band on a monthly retainer of $1,000 a month each, meaning they could quit playing shows and concentrate on their upcoming album. Their final show of 1990 was on New Year's Eve at the Satyricon in Portland, Oregon; the next day they drove back to Seattle for a session at the Music Source, produced by their soundman, Craig Montgomery who hoped that by working on the session he might put himself in the running to produce Nirvana's next

> "**I just started losing my inspiration to play. It shows. Ultimately I didn't give them much choice but to kick me out of the band.**"
>
> Chad Channing

album. The band recorded seven songs, revisiting 'Even In His Youth' and 'Token Eastern Song,' which they'd last recorded at the Music Source, along with five new songs, 'Aneurysm,' and early versions of 'Oh, The Guilt,' 'Radio Friendly Unit Shifter,' 'On A Plain,' and 'All Apologies,' the latter of which hadn't even been performed live. The session revealed Cobain's increasing refinement as a songwriter; while 'Aneurysm' and 'Radio Friendly' were hard rocking numbers, both 'On A Plain' and 'All Apologies' evidenced an ever-stronger pop sensibility, with irresistible hooks. Montgomery was also impressed by Grohl, saying "That tour was when I first met Dave. It was like a big breath of fresh air. He was young and fun and funny. He gave them a sound that took them over the top."

January also saw the release of the final Nirvana single on Sub Pop, a split single release with The Fluid, whose song 'Candy' appeared on one side of the disc; the other featured a live version of 'Molly's Lips,' recorded at a show in Portland in February 1990. The band performed just seven shows until they left for Los Angeles

in late April. At the April 17 show at Seattle's OK Hotel, they debuted a new song, 'Smells Like Teen Spirit,' which had developed out of a rehearsal jam. Though the song's lyrics weren't yet finished, it nonetheless made a powerful impression on the audience; "The place just exploded," Susie Tennant, a local publicity rep for DGC, remembered of the performance.

Sessions for Nirvana's major label debut began on May 2 at Sound City Studios in Van Nuys, a suburb of LA, the band moving in to an apartment complex nearby. The studio was then best known as the place where Fleetwood Mac recorded their landmark Rumours album; Cheap Trick, Pat Benatar, and Rick Springfield had also recorded at the studio, though Cobain was most impressed to learn motorcycle stuntman Evel Knievel had recorded his album *Evel Speaks To The Kids* at the studio.

After much discussion, the band had been able to secure Butch Vig, who'd produced the group the year before, as their producer. Recording went smoothly, in part because the band had worked on a

number of the songs with Vig before: 'Lithium,' 'In Bloom,' 'Breed,' and 'Stay Away.' 'Polly' was taken completely from the 1990 session. The other songs were new enough that Cobain was still tinkering with them lyrically; 'Drain You' had been written when Cobain and Grohl stopped off in San Francisco on the way to LA and recorded some tracks with Dale Crover and his then girlfriend, Debbie Shane. "Most of the songs were fairly finished," Vig recalls. "I don't know whether they played them live a lot, but I know that they did practice a lot. It wasn't like 'What are you playing here?' They knew."

Vig had been set to mix the record as well, but after hearing his early mixes, Nirvana's management and label suggested someone with "fresh ears" be brought in. Vig, who hadn't had a break between recording and mixing, agreed, and the band ultimately chose Andy Wallace for the job, due to his work with Slayer. By early June, the album was finished, and the band was back on the road on a short tour, after which they took a two-month break, little suspecting it would be quite some time before they'd be able to take a break again.

“ **That tour was when I first met Dave. It was like a big breath of fresh air. He was young and fun and funny. He gave them a sound that took them over the top.** ”

Craig Montgomery, Nirvana's sound engineer

NEVERMIND

How does one create an album that becomes a timeless classic? By not trying to. The members of Nirvana were confident about their material when they headed into Sound City Studios in May '91: "We knew that the stuff we were coming up with was catchy and cool and just good strong songs," Grohl later told Michael Azerrad. There was no grand plan to make an album that would be one of the biggest selling records of the decade, as well as a defining moment in rock music history. But that's exactly what happened. After the album's release in September 1991, the music scene was quickly divided into pre- and post-*Nevermind* eras.

The cover itself became equally iconic, with its shot of a baby swimming in water about to grab a dollar bill dangling enticingly on a fishhook. The idea was Cobain's. He'd long been interested in the reproductive process (in high school, he'd drawn a series of pictures of a sperm fertilizing an egg and developing into a baby), and a TV program about underwater birth had given him the visual idea, which he further tweaked by adding the dollar bill to the picture, thus creating a potent image of innocence on the verge of corruption.

Loss of innocence is a theme permeating the entire album as well, from the now instantly recognizable opening chords of 'Smells Like Teen Spirit' to the final sigh of depression in 'Something In The Way.' It's matched by a fierce anger, but there's never any feeling of triumph, of overcoming one's circumstances. But neither is it an album mired in despair. Even if the music's rage ultimately dissipates, it nonetheless provides a measure of release. And the sarcasm and self-deprecation running through the album keeps things from becoming too self-pitying.

'Teen Spirit' pulls this off all in one song. The opening guitar passage is one of those riffs you can listen to indefinitely, as the band apparently did as the song was coming together, jamming on the riff for over half an hour. After Cobain plays the riff solo, the song explodes as the full band comes in, scales back when Cobain sings the verses, and explodes again in the choruses. This constant building and releasing of tension gives the songs its edge, grabbing your attention and never letting go. Teasingly, Cobain shrugs off those who would look for a deeper meaning in the song, as well as his own apathy, in the final verse with a calculated "…whatever…never mind…" before ending the song by screaming

> **"I don't exactly know what 'Teen Spirit' means, but you know it means something, and it's intense as hell."**
>
> Butch Vig, *Nevermind* producer

> " We knew that
> the stuff we were
> coming up with
> was catchy and
> cool and just good
> strong songs. "
>
> Dave Grohl

OPPOSITE LEFT: Group shot, 1991. Note Krist's Dinosaur Jr. t-shirt; the band's guitarist, J. Mascis, was briefly considered as a possible drummer for Nirvana.

OPPOSITE RIGHT: The *Nevermind* album cover. The band members got the idea for the main image from watching a documentary about underwater birth; Kurt tweaked the picture further by adding the dollar bill dangling enticingly from a fishhook.

RIGHT: Tour poster for Nirvana's breakthrough series of concerts in the UK in 1991.

NIRVANA

BRISTOL BIERKELLER
MONDAY 4th NOVEMBER

LONDON ASTORIA
TUESDAY 5th NOVEMBER — SOLD OUT

WOLVERHAMPTON WULFRUN HALL
WEDNESDAY 6th NOVEMBER

BRADFORD UNIVERSITY
TUESDAY 26th NOVEMBER

BIRMINGHAM HUMMINGBIRD
WEDNESDAY 27th NOVEMBER

SHEFFIELD OCTAGON CENTRE
THURSDAY 28th NOVEMBER

EDINBURGH CARLTON STUDIOS
FRIDAY 29th NOVEMBER

GLASGOW QMU
SATURDAY 30th NOVEMBER

NEWCASTLE MAYFAIR
MONDAY 2nd DECEMBER

NOTTINGHAM ROCK CITY
TUESDAY 3rd DECEMBER

MANCHESTER ACADEMY
WEDNESDAY 4th DECEMBER

LONDON KILBURN NATIONAL
THURSDAY 5th DECEMBER

"A denial!" repeatedly. That we never know the target of this denial only adds to the song's mystery. "I don't exactly know what 'Teen Spirit' means," producer Vig told Rolling Stone, "but you know it means something, and it's intense as hell."

Cobain is similarly lyrically oblique throughout the album. 'Come As You Are' obscures the narrator's intentions in a series of contradictory statements. 'In Bloom' alternately derides and embraces the band's audience. 'On A Plain' cleverly hides whatever the narrator may really be thinking behind a welter of cryptic observations, admitting at one point that even he doesn't know what he's trying to say. Such lyrics provoked much debate about what the songs "really" meant. But the pull of the music is the album's greater strength. Some of 'Territorial Pissings' lyrics are outright clichés, yet the song works as a piece of brash punk playfulness, something that's also true of 'Stay Away.'

Irresistible hooks can be found throughout the album. Even 'Lounge Act,' generally considered one of *Nevermind*'s lesser tracks, has a strong melody and an equally compelling vocal from Cobain. The band finally perfected the punk/pop mix they'd been working toward from the beginning, a power trio who understood how to best use dynamics; when to go all out and when to hold back. This can be heard in Cobain's vocals as well, the howlings at the end of 'Stay Away' nicely contrasting with his dispassionate delivery in 'Polly,' a chilling tale of violence.

The album's pacing is also key to *Nevermind*'s appeal. 'Breed' pummels the listener with a barrage of noise, then neatly leads into the loping opening beat of 'Lithium.' The optimistic feel of 'On A Plain' gives way to the hopelessness of 'Something In The Way.' But there was a final joke awaiting the listener when, 10 minutes after the ending of 'Something In The Way,' the noise jam 'Endless, Nameless' bursts forth as a secret "hidden track," providing a bracing ending to an extraordinary album (though the number was inadvertently left off initial pressings of *Nevermind*).

Cobain would later disavow the record, though Vig, among others, attributes his reaction to the album's success: "As a punk, it's not cool to endorse an album that sells in the millions." But, as the last album Nirvana recorded out of the spotlight, it has a purity and a lack of self-consciousness that makes it the band's most fully realized musical statement. The music might have been of its time, but it was also built to last.

OPPOSITE: Some amusing advertising for *Nevermind*. This piece originates from Australia where the band endured huge popularity.

LEFT: After proving himself by working with Nirvana in April 1990, Butch Vig landed the job of producing the landmark album *Nevermind*.

BELOW: Promotional duties: Kurt and Dave busy signing a *Nevermind* poster and a skateboard. Note that Kurt, who was left-handed, is signing with his right hand.

FROM *NEVERMIND* TO 1992

Nirvana previewed a few songs from their upcoming album while on their brief tour in June '91, but the serious business of promoting the album really began in August. DGC had managed to sell over 100,000 copies of Sonic Youth's debut for the label, 1990's *Goo*, and label management was confident that Nirvana's fan base could lead to sales of at least half that.

LEFT: A rare in-store appearance at Tower Records, New York City, September 28, 1991.

BELOW: Kurt and Krist on stage during a concert at The Palace, Hollywood in October 1991.

On August 15, the band did an interview with Loyola Marymount University radio station KXLU in LA, during which the station debuted *Nevermind*'s first single, 'Smells Like Teen Spirit.' That evening, the band played a special industry showcase at the Roxy in LA; though designed for Geffen employees, the show had become a hot ticket and the venue was packed. The band members announced during the show they'd be shooting a video in two days and were looking for extras; flyers were also passed out to the audience. Due to the enthusiasm of the audience, a DGC vice president was heard confidently predicting *Nevermind* would surely sell 100,000 copies.

On August 17, the video for 'Teen Spirit' was filmed, directed by Sam Baker (who would go on to direct several impressive videos for Green Day's "comeback" album, *American Idiot*). Cobain had an elaborate concept for what he wanted to do with the video, but it was scaled back to being a (relatively) simple "pep rally from hell," as Grohl concisely put it; the band performing their song in a gloomy high school gymnasium, working the kids in the bleachers

into a frenzy that eventually sees them leaping from their seats and overwhelming the musicians. There were a few subversive touches, such as the cheerleaders wearing the "A" for anarchy symbol on their shirts. Cobain also insisted the video end with a close up of his face against Bayer's wishes; "[Kurt] wanted his fans to be able to look him directly in the eyes," Danny Goldberg, one of the band's managers, explained.

The next day the band flew overseas, where, after warm up dates in Ireland, they played a series of festivals in the UK (including the Reading Festival) and Europe. The shows were filmed by Dave Markey for his concert film *1991: The Year Punk Broke*, which also featured Sonic Youth, Dinosaur Jr., and the Ramones, among others. Since Nirvana weren't yet headliners, they played early in the day, then spent the rest of the time goofing off, drinking, and trashing their dressing rooms. It was all meant to be in good fun, signs of a playful attitude that Nirvana would continue to exhibit for the rest of the year.

ABOVE: Kurt, in his first appearance at the Reading Festival, 1991. Eugene Kelly, of the Vaselines, made a guest appearance when the band played 'Molly's Lips.'

BELOW: Novoselic in Tijuana, Mexico, on October 24, 1991.

RIGHT: Kurt Cobain performing live on stage, November 12, 1991 on the fall tour of that year.

Prior to returning to the States, the band taped another John Peel session on September 3. Though 'Teen Spirit' was due to be released the following week, the band instead performed 'Drain You' and 'Endless, Nameless' (the "hidden" track on *Nevermind*) and 'Dumb,' which had yet to be recorded (the show was broadcast November 19). The band sounded somewhat tired, but did manage to extend 'Endless, Nameless' for nearly nine minutes — an accurate audio depiction of the closing frenzy of their shows, which usually saw them smashing their instruments.

Back in the US, there was a record release party on Friday, September 13 at Seattle club Re-bar (the invites read "*Nevermind* Triskaidekaphobia," the "phobia" in question being a fear of Friday the 13th), where the band became embroiled in a food fight and were momentarily ejected from their own record release party. The next day, the 'Teen Spirit' video made its debut on MTV on *120 Minutes*, their alternative rock show, a sign that Nirvana was still regarded as something of fringe act – for the moment (the single eventually reached #6 US, #7 UK). On the 16th, the band made an in-store appearance at Seattle record shop Beehive Music & Video, which drew a line around the block hours before the show had even started. On September 20, they began a North American tour.

Nevermind was released on September 23 in the UK, September 24 in the US. As the tour had been booked before the record's release, the band played clubs and theaters, which, as their popularity grew, were sold out and sometimes dangerously overcrowded. Meanwhile, *Nevermind* entered Billboard's "Top

200" album chart at 144; a month later, it was in the Top 40. MTV moved 'Teen Spirit' to its "Buzz Bin," which further boosted sales. When Butch Vig saw the band play Chicago, "The buzz in the air was unbelievable," he recalls. "Kids were screaming and crying, and almost everyone already knew the lyrics. I was thinking, 'Wow, I might eventually have a gold record,' and of course it went gold in a matter of weeks."

During the tour, Nirvana played a Rock For Choice benefit in Los Angeles on October 25; though not an overtly political band, they championed various progressive causes throughout their career. The same day, Cobain and Novoselic taped an appearance on MTV's *Headbanger's Ball*, with Cobain playfully wearing a bright yellow gown for the occasion; "I'm dressed for the ball," he drawled to host Riki Rachtman's bafflement, going to joke that Novoselic hadn't bothered to give him a corsage. Playing along, Novoselic responded, "At least I asked you out!"

The North American tour ended on Halloween in Seattle, with the band playing the Paramount Theatre and their friends Mudhoney and Bikini Kill opening. The show was being filmed, so the band arranged for two of their friends from Olympia to serve as on-stage dancers, the young man wearing a shirt reading "Girl," and a young woman wearing a shirt reading "Boy," another playful piece of subversion; clips from the show later appeared in the 'Lithium' video and the long-form video *Live! Tonight! Sold Out!!*

And then it was back to the UK and Europe, where the level of excitement about the band was just as intense; a cover headline on the *New Musical Express* lauded them as "The Guns N' Roses It's Okay To Like." In addition to live shows, Nirvana made three appearances on UK television over the next month, beginning on November 8 with *The Word*, their first appearance on live TV. Prior to playing 'Teen Spirit,' Cobain announced, "I'd like all of the you people in this room to know that Courtney Love, the lead singer of the sensational pop group Hole, is the best fuck in the world," referring to his new girlfriend. That naturally provoked comment, and the band happily upped the stakes on their next TV appearance, a taping for *Top of the Pops* on November 27, when they were told they'd be miming instrumentally to 'Teen Spirit' with Cobain providing a live vocal. The band agreed, but in addition to miming deliberately poorly, Cobain delivered the song in a deep bass voice, while pretending to fellate his microphone. The producers asked for a retake, but the band refused. "At this time their thinking when they were on stage was 'What could we do that would be funny?'" explains soundman Craig Montgomery.

Their final TV appearance during the tour was on December 6 on *Tonight With Jonathan Ross*. The group obligingly rehearsed 'Lithium,' but during the show tore into a furious version of 'Territorial Pissings,' ending with Cobain knocking his mic stand over and Novoselic throwing his bass into Grohl's drum kit, which Grohl promptly kicked over. Host Ross got a laugh by noting Nirvana was available for "playing children's birthday parties and bar mitzvahs."

The band was not so unpredictable in their final radio appearances, though they still declined to promote their new single. On November 9 they taped a performance for BBC Radio 1's Mark Goodier's *Evening Session*, performing solid versions of 'Polly,' 'Something In The Way,' 'Been A Son,' and 'Aneurysm,' a 'Teen Spirit' B-side. The show was broadcast November 18. Their last radio appearance, recorded on November 25, was for Dutch radio stations VPRO and VARA. The band was noticeably tired by this point, and only managed to record two numbers, 'Where Did You Sleep Last Night' and 'Here She Comes Now,' along with a long jam.

The constant touring was beginning to wear on the band, as Jack Endino noted that evening, when Nirvana played a show at Amsterdam's Paradiso club. Endino's own band, Skin Yard, had just finished a tour of Europe and he stopped by to see Nirvana's show. "Kurt wasn't doing too good," he recalls. "There were all these people with cameras and movie cameras on the stage, and he was a little out of tune and he was very angry at these cameras: 'Get the hell off my stage!' And backstage he was really uneasy, he looked really pale. Everybody seemed to be really uneasy and very unhappy. Like suddenly the success was starting to bother them because people were starting to come at them. Suddenly people wouldn't leave them alone."

In later recalling the tour for Michael Azerrad's *Come As You Are*, the band made their discomfort obvious. "I just remember being real miserable and starving and sick all the time," said Cobain, while Novoselic admitted his drinking was such that "A few shows I barely remember playing…I was stressed out." As Grohl summed it up, "I was insane. I was out of my fucking mind. I was sick of playing, sick of it." As a result, a week of dates was cancelled, allowing for a longer break before the band was expected back on the road.

On December 27, Nirvana began a short tour which also featured Pearl Jam and the Red Hot Chili Peppers. The Chili Peppers were the ostensible headliners, but Nirvana's success was about to escalate even higher. On the last night of the tour, January 2, 1992 in Salem, Oregon, Nirvana learned that *Nevermind* was about to top the album charts in America.

OPPOSITE LEFT: Krist Novoselic on stage in Germany. "Some dates I barely remember playing," Krist said of Nirvana's fall 1991 European tour.

OPPOSITE RIGHT: Performing live in Tijuana, Mexico, October 1991. One reviewer noted that this show in Tijuana was a particularly violent gig on Nirvana's 1991 North American tour.

BELOW: The band rehearsing in San Francisco, October 1991.

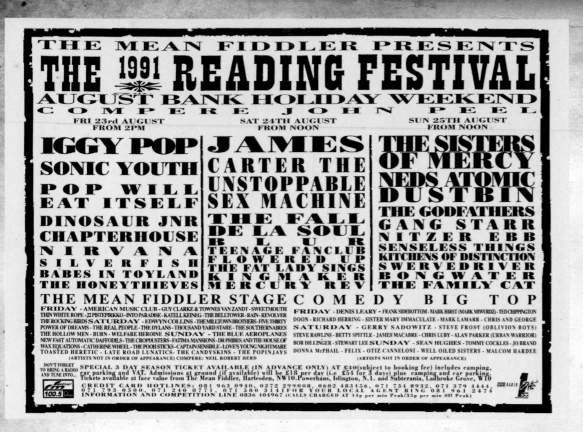

> " I was insane. I was out of my fucking mind. I was sick of playing, sick of it. "

Dave Grohl

NIRVANA

> **"I just remember being real miserable and starving and sick all the time."**
>
> Kurt Cobain

–You Are Cordially Invited–
Nirvana – acoustic concert
Thursday, October 24 (time t.b.a.)
"Come As you Are"
Off the Record III   298-4755
3865 5th Ave. San Diego 92103

OFF THE RECORD
3865 FIFTH AVE.
SAN DIEGO, CA 92103

D C G PROMOTIONS presents....

NIRVANA

VENUE — Conor Hall

DATE — Mon 9 Dec   ADMISSION £6.50

TIME — 8pm

CONDITIONS OF SALE

No Alcohol; No Refunds; No Readmission; No Cameras or Recorders. Ticket Holder assumes all risk of injury and all responsibility for property loss, destruction or theft and releases the Promoters from all liability therefor. This ticket is not to be resold; any violation will render it invalid.

No · 8738

VIP

ROMANTIC ROSE

TEEN Spirit ANTI-PERSPIRANT

by **lady stick**

NIRVANA

ABOVE: A rare ticket from a concert in Belfast, Northern Ireland's Conor Hall.

ABOVE RIGHT: An invite to see the band perform acoustically in-store at San Diego's Off The Record.

RIGHT: A VIP backstage pass.

KRIST NOVOSELIC

Krist Novoselic's position as bass player in Nirvana mirrored his non-musician role in the band as well - providing the kind of rock solid support that holds everything together. Although Novoselic played with other musicians around Aberdeen, it was Kurt Cobain with whom he formed his strongest musical, and personal bond.

Krist Anthony Novoselic was born on May 16, 1965 in Compton, California, and grew up in Gardena, 12 miles south of Los Angeles. His parents, Krist and Maria, were both Croatian immigrants, and Novoselic became fluent in both English and Croatian as he grew up (for a time, he Anglicized his first name to "Chris," but in the wake of the Bosnian conflict in the early '90s, he reverted to the Croatian spelling). He learned to play the accordion as a child, then moved on to guitar in his teens. But when he finally began practicing regularly with Cobain, he switched to bass.

As the only member of Nirvana who graduated from high school, Novoselic handled the band's managerial duties until they acquired formal management. His relentless scouring of thrift shops led him to the song that eventually become Nirvana's first single, when he purchased the Shocking Blue album that contained the song 'Love Buzz' (he also kept an eye open during such excursions for any workable left-handed guitars that Cobain, a lefty, might be able to use). On Nirvana's early tours, he kept such a close eye on the band's finances he mandated that to save on fuel, the van's air conditioning could not be turned on, even when traveling through the Southwest – in July.

But of course, Novoselic's most important contribution to Nirvana was as the group's bassist. "A lot of the hooks in the songs, Krist was writing on bass," says producer Butch Vig. "I think Kurt basically let him come up with his own parts. They're great hooks." From the beginning, he supplied the sound that helped make tracks like 'Floyd The Barber' and 'Paper Cuts' become so exceptionally heavy. But what he called his "walking pop song bass line" gave a light touch to such songs as 'About A Girl,' 'Sliver,' and 'Lithium.' He even found a way to put his childhood accordion skills to good use. Novoselic had picked up an accordion as Nirvana rehearsed for their Unplugged appearance, then realized that 'Jesus Doesn't Want Me For A Sunbeam' would be the perfect place to make use of the instrument.

After Nirvana became successful, Novoselic became increasingly interested in politics. He'd always been the one to make the occasional political comment at shows, and now he had a larger platform from which to air his views. During a break in Nirvana's schedule in 1992, he was asked to come to a rally at the Washington state capitol in protest of a so-called "Erotic Music" bill, under which music retailers could face prosecution for selling music that was deemed "offensive." It was his first step into a larger political arena. "I wasn't prepared to say anything," he recalls. "And all of a sudden all these cameras are on me. I didn't realize they'd

OPPOSITE LEFT: Nirvana often promoted their favorite bands on their t-shirts. *Black Candy* is an album by Olympia band Beat Happening.

OPPOSITE RIGHT: Though he's also a guitarist, Krist opted to switch to bass when he and Kurt founded Nirvana.

RIGHT: Always keenly interested in current events, Krist was the most likely to make politically-oriented comments during Nirvana's shows.

ABOVE: Krist at one of the last shows he played with Flipper, one of his early influences, on September 5, 2008.

RIGHT: Kurt Cobain, Krist Novoselic and Dave Grohl in Germany, November 12, 1991.

be on me because Nirvana was so popular at the moment. It was definitely a good lesson about the power."

After Nirvana came to an end, Novoselic increasingly divided his time between musical projects and political endeavors. Sometimes he was able to do both at the same time, as when he founded JAMPAC (Joint Artists and Music Promotions Political Action Committee), which lobbied for the music industry's interests, or put together a one-off band, The No WTO Combo, which formed to protest the World Trade Organization's Seattle conference in 1999. The group, which also consisted of Dead Kennedys' lead singer Jello Biafra, Soundgarden guitarist Kim Thayil, and drummer Gina Mainwal, released an album of their sole show, *Live From The Battle In Seattle*, in 2000. Most recently, he's spoken frequently about electoral reform, serving as chair of FairVote, an organization that works extensively on the issue. His book on the subject, *Of Grunge and Government: Let's Fix This Broken Democracy!*, was published in 2004.

Novoselic's musical outfits haven't been bound by convention either. His first post-Nirvana band, Sweet 75, mixed alternative rock with Latin folk music, courtesy of the trio's Venezuelan lead singer, Yva Las Vegas (the group's self-titled album was released in 1997). His next band, Eyes Adrift, another trio that featured the Meat Puppets' Curt Kirkwood and Bud Gaugh from Sublime, created what might be called alt-country space rock, as evidenced by their self-titled album, released in 2002. In 2006, he joined Flipper for a two-year stint, a band he credited with originally getting him into punk rock; he appears on the group's 2009 albums *Love* and *Fight*.

Though not in a band at time of writing, Novoselic has written columns on music for the *Seattle Weekly* blog, and serves as a DJ for Astoria, Oregon-based radio station KMUN. Now living on a farm in southwest Washington with his second wife, Novoselic's options for future projects are wide open – just the way he likes it.

1992

Nevermind grabbing the top position on *Billboard*'s Top Pop Albums chart on January 11, 1992, was seen as an indication of a sea change in the music industry. A band that was unknown outside alternative rock circles had sold over two million copies of their major label debut in the US in less than four months. *Nevermind* had knocked Michael Jackson's *Dangerous* from #1, and peaked at #1 in numerous other countries as well (though oddly, in the UK, where the band had always enjoyed strong support, the album only reached #7). There were an increasing number of bands from the underground signing to major labels - indeed, other Seattle bands like Alice In Chains and Soundgarden had signed with major labels before Nirvana – but no one had such an out-of-the-box success as Nirvana had.

Unfortunately, there was another new element that would make 1992 a very fraught year in the band's career. In late 1990, Cobain had begun using heroin, and it now became increasingly obvious he'd developed quite a serious problem. The media had also begun to get wind of the situation. Jerry McCulley of *BAM* (*Bay Area Magazine*) had interviewed Cobain during the late December tour, and his subsequent article, published in January, noted that Cobain repeatedly nodded off during the interview, and that his "pinned pupils; sunken cheeks; and scabbed, sallow skin suggest something more than serious than mere fatigue."

Everyone around Cobain was distressed about the situation, but there was a lot of promotional work to get through before the problem could be addressed with; for the moment, journalists were told Cobain's appearance was due to fatigue and his recurring stomach problems. The band flew to New York the second week of January and taped a nine-song set for MTV before a live audience on

ABOVE LEFT: Nirvana was able to book a number of their favorite acts when they played the Reading Festival on August 30, 1992, including Mudhoney, L-7, The Melvins, and ABBA impersonators Bjorn Again.

ABOVE: A backstage pass from the Reading Festival.

TOUR 92

INSET: Krist Novoselic on stage in Sydney, Australia in February 1992.

LEFT: Kurt looking menacing during a high-energy live performance.

FAR LEFT: A commemorative scarf from Nirvana's 1992 tour.

January 10. The next night they appeared as the musical act on the popular comedy show Saturday Night Live, performing 'Teen Spirit' and 'Territorial Pissings.' Cobain didn't look well, his eyes shut for most of the performance, but he was nonetheless compelling. The band also strove to promote some of their favorite alternative acts during the show, Cobain wearing a homemade Flipper shirt, Grohl wearing a Melvins shirt, and Novoselic wearing a Melvins shirt during 'Teen Spirit' and an L7 shirt during 'Territorial Pissings.' To further tweak the audience, during the closing sequence, when cast and guests come on stage to wave goodbye, Novoselic kissed both Ghrol and Cobain on the lips.

Cobain returned to LA, where he was living with Courtney Love, now his fiancé. Nirvana's managers then staged an intervention, which, according to Danny Goldberg, was unsuccessful. But Love learned she was pregnant, and she and Cobain had a doctor help them through a private detox at a motel. It marked the first a number of times Cobain would attempt to quit heroin.

From January 19 to 22, Nirvana shot a video for their latest single, 'Come As You Are' (which reached #32 US, #9 UK). Cobain asked director Kevin Kerslake to hide his face, as he was tired of being recognized, and Kerslake created a dreamy piece of work, with cascading water blurring the band's facial features through most of the video (though Cobain teasingly kissed the camera lens at the end).

On January 24, the band began a Pacific Rim tour, which took in Australia, Japan, and two dates in Honolulu, Hawaii. A special EP, *Hormoaning*, was released to tie in with the tour, containing the songs from the 1990 John Peel session, along with 'Aneurysm' and 'Even In His Youth.' Cobain's stomach problems returned, resulting in one show being cancelled; he later discovered the pain pills a doctor provided him contained methadone, getting him addicted once more to opiates. But the tour struggled on, Cobain eventually well enough to agree to a cover shoot for Rolling Stone magazine, wearing a t-shirt that defiantly proclaimed "Corporate magazines still suck." Two days after the tour's completion, on February 24, Cobain and Love wed on the beach in front of their hotel, the Hilton Hawaiian Village.

The band members wouldn't see each again until April. An argument over songwriting royalties nearly split the band at the time. The royalties had been split equally, but now Cobain wanted to receive a bigger share as he wrote most of the music and all of the lyrics. Novoselic and Grohl had no problem with this, but Cobain added he wanted the split to be applied retroactively. Novoselic and Grohl eventually agreed.

On April 7 the band got back together in Seattle for a quick session at the Laundry Room – a studio in the home Grohl was sharing with his friend, Barrett Jones, who produced the session. For a moment, personal problems were forgotten, as the band buzzed through 'Return of the Rat,' set for a Wipers tribute album released that June, 'Curmudgeon,' destined as the B-side for their next single, and 'Oh, The Guilt,' which wouldn't be released until the following year. "I don't think they'd ever really played the songs before," says Jones. "But they figured them out pretty quick. I think they were trying to be a little more punk rock about the whole thing. Trying to get away from the *Nevermind* glossiness. They wanted to be as low budget as possible about it."

It was hoped that the band would undertake a US stadium tour, but Cobain insisted he needed a break and spent the next few months in LA. He entered a formal rehab program, but failed to complete it and was soon back on the drug. Novoselic and Grohl got involved with other projects, uncertain how to deal with the

RIGHT: Due to rumours about his health, Kurt jokingly wore a hospital gown when he was wheeled onstage (by *Melody Maker* journalist Everett True) for Nirvana's appearance at the Reading Festival.

FAR RIGHT: Footage from Nirvana's 1992 Reading Festival performance was finally officially released on DVD in 2009.

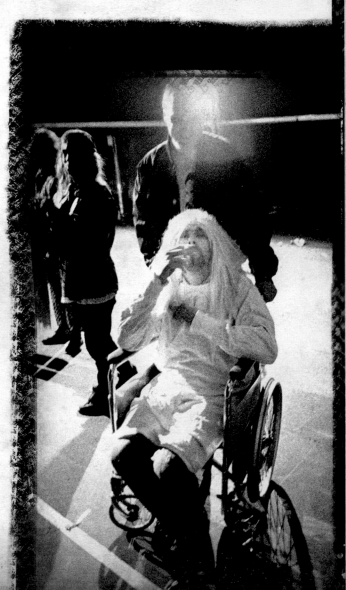

ABOVE: Nirvana at the MTV Video Music Awards, September 9, 1992. The band won awards for Best New Band and Best Alternative Video for 'Smells Like Teen Spirit.'

> ## " Pinned pupils; sucken cheeks; and scabbed, sallow skin suggest something more serious than mere fatigue."
>
> Jerry McCulley of *Bay Area Magazine* on Kurt Cobain

situation. "It was hard to understand," Novoselic told Michael Azzerad. "I couldn't get over the whole hurdle of heroin."

In June, Nirvana embarked on a 10-date swing through the UK and Europe. Cobain was now on methadone, but his stomach problems flared up again, and drug rumours continued. Love accompanied the band on tour, and when she began to experience contractions, the rest of the tour was cancelled after a July 4 date in Bilbao, Spain. The same month saw the release of 'Lithium,' which reached the Top 20 in the UK, though it failed to crack the US Top 40 (it did appear in Billboard's Mainstream and Modern Rock charts). For the video, Kevin Kerslake compiled tour footage from various shows.

Cobain again entered rehab after returning from the tour. Love also checked into the hospital, suffering from exhaustion. Their daughter was born on August 18, and named Frances Bean Cobain – "Frances" after Frances McKee of The Vaselines, and "Bean" because Cobain thought the baby looked like a bean in her sonogram. But the couple's happiness over their daughter's healthy birth was short-lived. A *Vanity Fair* profile on Love, published that same month, created uproar when it suggested Love continued taking heroin after learning she was pregnant (an accusation Love has always denied).

In the midst of this turmoil, Nirvana still had stage engagements to fulfill. They made a triumphant appearance at the Reading Festival on August 30, with Cobain poking fun at the rumors about his health by being brought on stage in a wheelchair wearing a hospital gown. The show was as powerful as the shows in the fall of '91 had been, making it clear Nirvana was not about to break up.

Back in the US, the band appeared on the MTV Video Music Awards on September 9. There was yet another controversy when the band said they wanted to play a new number, 'Rape Me,' which MTV strenuously opposed. They eventually agreed to perform 'Lithium,' and collected awards for Best Alternative

LEFT: Dave, October 4, 1992, when Nirvana was a surprise opening act for Mudhoney at Seattle's Crocodile Café.

"It was hard to understand, I couldn't get over the whole hurdle of heroin."

Krist Novoselic

LEFT: A photograph of the band by Karen Blair. She was close to the band and photographed them many times.

Music Video (for 'Teen Spirit') and Best New Artist. They then returned to the Pacific Northwest, headlining benefit shows in Portland, Oregon on September 10, and Seattle on September 11. In October, they made two unexpected small show appearances as the surprise opening act for Mudhoney at Western Washington University in Bellingham on October 3, and Seattle's Crocodile Café on October 4. Out of the spotlight, the band relaxed and clearly had a good time at the gigs.

October was a busy month. On the 15th, the band returned to LA to shoot a video for their next single, 'In Bloom,' in which they donned identical suits in the fashion of early '60s pop groups, footage intercut with shots of the band wearing dresses and tearing down the set. On October 25 a recording session was held at Seattle's Word of Mouth studio (formerly Reciprocal) to record demos for the band's upcoming album. To producer Jack Endino's surprise, Cobain didn't show up for hours, his absence shrugged off with the comment "You get used to this when you're dealing with Kurt." He did appear on time the next night, and the band recorded several instrumentals, along with 'Rape Me.' "But it was really nothing whatsoever like the band that I had worked with," Endino notes.

The band's mood was no better when they performed a one-off gig on October 30 in Buenos Aires, Argentina. Cobain was incensed at the rude reception the opening act, Calamity Jane (friends from his days in Olympia) had received, and his anger was evident in his performance; at one point, he simply walked off the stage. It was a dispiriting end for what was Nirvana's last live show of the year.

But it was also soon forgotten in the rush up to the holidays. 'In Bloom' gave the band another hit, and the fans got another present in the form of *Incesticide*, an album of early and unreleased tracks. It had been a most hectic year, but now it was time to get back to work.

INCESTICIDE

Incesticide served two purposes. It allowed DGC a way to make some more money out of their of hottest property when they failed to deliver a new album in 1992. But more importantly, it gave those who arrived late to the Nirvana party a chance to play catch-up, offering a concise summary of the band's career up to the point of the groundbreaking *Nevermind* and tossing in a few rarities to boot.

Five tracks dated all the way back to the band's January 1988 demo, featuring Dale Crover on drums. 'Downer' already appeared on the CD version of *Bleach*, but only hardcore fans were likely to have heard 'Mexican Seafood,' previously released on C/Z Records' *Teriyaki Asthma* compilations (a 1989 EP and 1991 LP). The song lurches along to Cobain's continual groaning, and features one of his most graphic and unpleasant lyrics about the nature of illness. 'Beeswax' had appeared on Kill Rock Stars' self-titled compilation, released in 1991, another jaggedly rhythmic song with a rambling, stream-of-consciousness lyric, providing the clearest illustration of how Cobain had developed as a songwriter; in stark contrast, some later songs would feature little more than a single verse and chorus, which he'd then simply repeat.

But both 'Hairspray Queen' or 'Aero Zeppelin' make their official debut on this album. 'Hairspray Queen' is most obviously musically influenced by early '80s new wave, while Cobain indulges himself in a number of vocal stylings, from wild-cat screaming to his later familiar drawl. 'Aero Zeppelin' sends up the pretensions of arena rock acts and their sheep-like fans, eager to follow any latest trend. For a band whose members had all grown up listening to '70s hard rock, it was an easy musical homage to pull off.

'Big Long Now' was a true rarity, a genuine *Bleach* outtake that the band had essentially forgotten as soon as they'd recorded it; they declined to put it on *Bleach*, feeling the album already had enough "slow and heavy" songs, and they rarely played it live. But Endino had been impressed with Cobain's vocal, which has a strength not heard on most of *Bleach*'s songs, and reminded the band of the track's existence when *Incesticide* was being compiled. It's a powerful performance that would probably have worked better on *Bleach* than other "slow and heavy" songs like 'Sifting.'

From this point on, Nirvana's pop leanings become more pronounced. In 'Stain,' recorded in 1989, Cobain strips himself back lyrically as well; 'Stain' is one of those single-verse-and-chorus songs. Of more interest is a clever lyrical touch; though Cobain sings the verse in third person, he switches to first person in the chorus, taking what seems a harsh observation of a poor loser and turning it back in on himself, with the poppy melody keeping the mood light. The pop quotient is pushed up even further on 'Sliver,' released as a single in 1990, and one of the most straightforward

RIGHT: These photos were taken during a Dutch radio session on November 25, 1991. While songs from the band's radio sessions have appeared on releases like *Incesticide*, no songs from this Dutch session have been officially released.

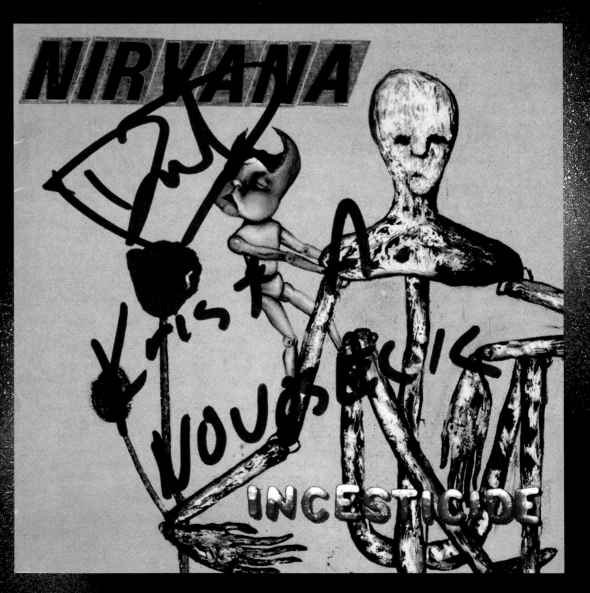

ABOVE: A copy of *Incesticide*, autographed by Dave and Krist. The cover art was by Kurt.

songs Cobain ever wrote, taking an incident from his childhood and transforming it into something nostalgic but utterly lacking in sentiment. The single's flip side, 'Dive,' was a template for the songs on *Nevermind*, with its thick guitars welded to a catchy melody, and Cobain's raw vocals, culminating in an impressive scream leading into the chorus.

The rest of the album is given over to tracks from BBC radio sessions in 1990 and 1991. The 1990 session (three songs of which appear here) is especially interesting as it consisted entirely of covers, giving some insight into the band's influences; unlike other bands, especially in their early years, Nirvana's shows rarely included covers. Cobain was an unabashed Vaselines fan, crediting the band with providing "a reminder of how much I really value innocence and children and my youth," and Nirvana's covers of 'Molly's Lips' and 'Son of a Gun' are breezy and playful. Devo's 'Turnaround' is darker, but no less freewheeling.

The remaining songs are from a 1991 BBC session. Nirvana themselves preferred the '91 version of 'Been A Son,' which has a more polished performance than the '89 studio version recorded

with Steve Fisk, but 'Aneurysm' is less powerful than the '91 studio version recorded with Craig Montgomery, particularly in the devastating howl Cobain unleashes at the end of the studio version. The title addendum '(New Wave) Polly' refers to the fact that for this version the band ups the tempo and manages to bring the song in at under two minutes, showing if nothing else that the band didn't regard the studio versions of songs as sacrosanct.

At the time of its release, *Incesticide* attracted more attention for its Cobain-written liner notes which attacked what he saw as the exploitative side of the music industry, and invited any of the band's fans who were homophobic, racist, or sexist to "Please do this one favor for us – leave us the fuck alone!" One of his paintings was used for the cover, underscoring his apparently gloomy mindset. But the music within is far from dispirited; it's the sound of a band searching, and at last finding, their own distinctive voice.

RIGHT: 'Beeswax,' from Nirvana's first professional demo, initially appeared on this *Kill Rock Stars* compilation.

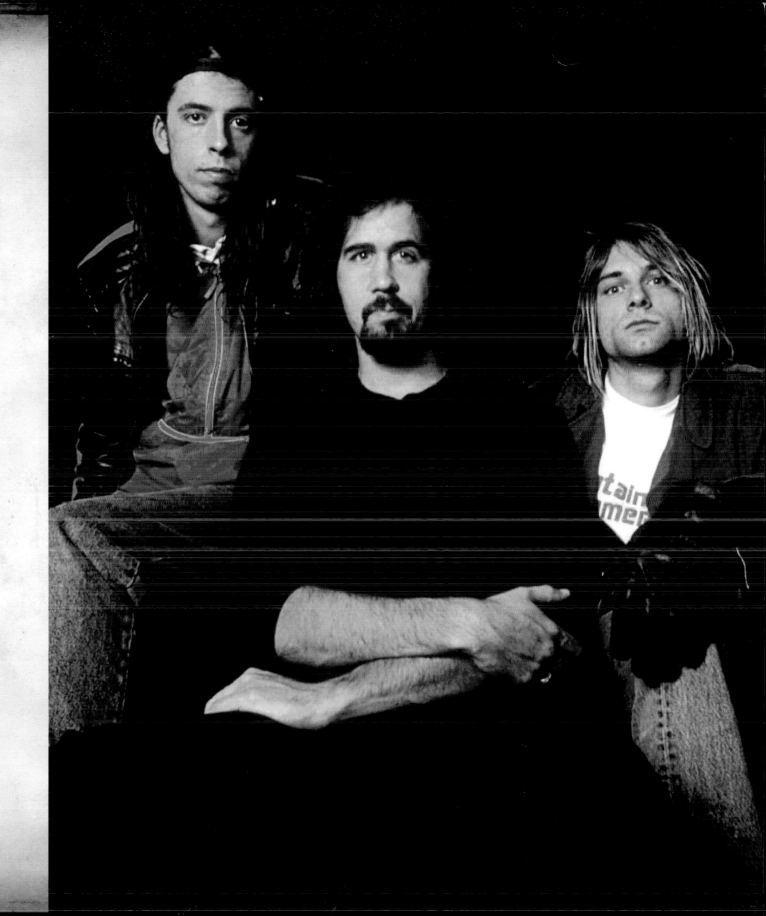

> **"Please do this one favor for us – leave us the f**k alone!"**
>
> Kurt Cobain

OPPOSITE: A group shot from the Dutch radio session in November 1991.

RIGHT: Looking sombre. Nirvana as photographed by Karen Blair.

As 1993 began, the most pressing issue facing Nirvana was recording a new album. Songs had slowly been coming together over the previous year. Haphazard though it may have been, the demo session with Jack Endino the previous October showed that the musical arrangements for at least six songs had been worked out, and the band had been rehearsing other songs as well.

But first up was a trip to Brazil. On January 16, the band played a show in Sao Paulo, the first of two shows which were part of the Hollywood Rock Festival. The band was in a strange mood, breaking off to play snippets of modern pop like Kim Wilde's 'Kids In America' and Duran Duran's 'Rio.' "It felt like a drunken party, something you would see in the basement," the band's guitar tech, Earnie Bailey, recalled. At one point, Novoselic walked off in frustration, though he was persuaded to go back on stage; if the band didn't play their allotted time, they wouldn't get paid. At the conclusion of their set, the band destroyed "everything in sight," according to Bailey.

They next went to Rio de Janeiro, where they entered BMG Ariola Discos Ltda. studios to work on more demos, with soundman Craig Montgomery producing. They put the most effort into 'Heart-Shaped Box,' a song that had been coming together at soundchecks. "You could tell that this was an important song in a lot of ways," says Bailey. 'Scentless Apprentice' was another strong effort, a song Montgomery recalls as being a favorite of the band's, noting "Every chance they got they played this song – at soundcheck, in the studio." Indeed, the band played both 'Heart-Shaped Box' and 'Scentless Apprentice' at the São Paulo show.

'Scentless Apprentice' had a harsh edge to it, as did the subsequent numbers, which also had an improvisational feel; to Montgomery, it almost seemed as if the band was making them up on the spot. While the songs 'Milk It,' 'Moist Vagina,' 'I Hate Myself And Want To Die,' and 'Very Ape' had some structure, 'Gallons Of Rubbing Alcohol Flow Through The Strip' and the number belatedly entitled 'The Other Improv' were lengthy jams, providing some indication of what band rehearsals may have been like. Grohl then showed off his multi-instrumental skills on a cover of Unleashed's 'Onward Into Countless Battles,' a frantic metal romp with the sole lyric "Meat!" The session concluded with a cover of Terry Jacks' 'Seasons In The Sun,' a somewhat morbid number about a young man facing an early death. It was one of the first singles Cobain bought, and though he didn't get all the lyrics right, there's a still a poignant quality in his mournful delivery.

The second Hollywood Rocks Festival show came on January 23, also in Rio. The band was in much better form, with 'Scentless Apprentice' going off into a jam that lasted 20 minutes, and featured Cobain roaming around the stage, eventually dropping his guitar and dancing in front of one of the cameras filming the show. His face expressionless, he opened his trousers, then mimed jerking off into the camera (the shot cuts away to a side view at this point), and, in a final display of contempt, caressed the lens, before spitting directly into it.

ABOVE: Kurt and his beloved daughter, Frances Bean Cobain in late 1992. Those who knew him often talked about what a devoted father Kurt was.

RIGHT: A pass for MTV's *Live and Loud* show, taped on December 13, 1993 in Seattle, with Nirvana headlining.

FAR RIGHT: A photo session during the promotion of *In Utero*, July 24, 1993, New York City.

OPPOSITE: Nirvana on *Saturday Night Live*, September 25, 1993. The band performed 'Heart-Shaped Box' and 'Rape Me.'

MTV
MUSIC TELEVISION

Live & Loud
Seattle, WA

TALENT GUEST

TAR

NOT VALID WITHOUT SIGNATURE

The following month Nirvana finally headed into the studio to work on their second album for DGC. Cobain was especially anxious that their next record should avoid what he called the "candy ass" sound of *Nevermind.* He wanted a raw, authentically punk sound, and the decision to work with iconoclastic producer Steve Albini seemed to ensure that. Albini had been a member of the bands Big Black (Cobain had seen the group's final performance in 1987, at an abandoned steam plant in Seattle) and the controversially named Rapeman; as a producer, he worked with two acts Cobain very much admired, the Pixies and PJ Harvey.

There had in fact already been speculation in the UK press that Albini was going to produce the next Nirvana album, to the point that Albini issued a denial; a day later, he was formally approached by the band's management. After talking with Cobain and Grohl, he agreed to take the job; "It seemed like they wanted to make precisely the sort of record that I'm comfortable doing, and it seemed like they genuinely liked the records that I did make," he explains. He was also assured he could work directly with the band, and not have to deal with their label.

Sessions were set up at Pachyderm Studios, located outside of Cannon Falls, Minnesota (40 miles from Minneapolis) to cut down on distractions (Novoselic described the setting as being "cooped up in the middle of nowhere, like a gulag"). The band arrived ready and eager to work. Though half of songs recorded had been around for over a year, and the band had demoed all of but one of the songs

that ended up on the album ('Serve The Servants'), Cobain was still tinkering with the lyrics. Sessions began on February 13 and basic tracks were completed by the 16th; the remaining 10 days were spent on recording Cobain's vocals, and mixing. Courtney Love came by for a short stay, and there was some tension around the visit. But overall the sessions went smoothly. Albini was impressed with the "sprawling and aimless" quality of the songs, in contrast to the more structured work on *Nevermind,* and the band felt they'd created an inspired, and challenging, work.

Once the sessions were over, there was little band business until the release of the album, entitled *In Utero* (Cobain had also considered "I Hate Myself And Want To Die", a sarcastic comment on his condition), in September. In March, the band filmed a video for 'Sliver,' ostensibly to promote the *Incesticide* set. Again directed by Kevin Kerslake, the video was shot in Cobain's garage at his Seattle home; Cobain and Love had left LA in early 1993.

In April, Nirvana played a show in San Francisco, a benefit for the Croatian-based Tresnjevka Women's Group (set up to aid survivors of Bosnian War). In July, they appeared at the New Music Seminar in New York City; in August, the band played their final date as a trio, a Seattle show benefiting the Mia Zapata Investigative Fund (Zapata, lead singer of Seattle band the Gits, had been murdered in July; her killer was arrested and convicted a decade later).

There had been a minor controversy over the mixing of *In Utero.* The band's management and label had found the aggressive,

BELOW LEFT: An outtake from the photo-shoot for *The Advocate,* a US gay publication, January 1, 1993 at the Four Seasons Hotel in Seattle. Kurt was on the cover of the February 9, 1993 issue.

BELOW: Kurt began wearing hunting caps in 1993, and was often seen with one when he went around Seattle. Ostensibly a disguise, they actually drew more attention to him.

raw recording too rough for their tastes. The band members were initially resistant, but eventually came around to the same view. Albini was offered the chance to do another mix, but declined, telling the band he thought he'd done the best he could. Scott Litt was brought in to remix 'Heart-Shaped Box' and 'All Apologies,' and the mix was further smoothed out during the mastering process. The news then reached the press, resulting in enough articles about the band being "pressured" by their label to change their music that they were forced to issue a denial, Cobain quoted as saying in a press release, "We have 100% control of our music!"

At the end of August, Nirvana shot a video to accompany *In Utero*'s first single, 'Heart-Shaped Box' (which featured 'Milk It' and an *In Utero* outtake, Grohl's 'Marigold,' as B-sides). The video, directed by Dutch photographer/filmmaker Anton Corbijn, was filled with disturbing imagery, like an angelic blonde girl in a Ku Klux Klan robe, and an old man being crucified while wearing a Santa Claus

hat; at the video's end, the band is seen waiting in a hospital room as the old man dies. Cobain later told Corbijn that out of all Nirvana's videos, this came the closest to what he originally envisioned.

On September 2, the band was in the audience at that year's MTV Music Video Awards, with 'In Bloom' winning Best Alternative Video. *In Utero* was released on September 14 in the UK, and September 21 in the US, topping the charts in both countries. On September 25, the band appeared on Saturday Night Live again, performing 'Heart-Shaped Box' and 'Rape Me,' along with debuting their new guitarist, Pat Smear, from LA punk band the Germs.

A US tour began the next month on October 18 in Phoenix, Arizona. It was the band's first arena tour, with Smear's presence as second guitarist helping Cobain concentrate on his vocals. More *In Utero* outtakes popped up on other releases: 'Verse Chorus Verse' on the *No Alternative* compilation, 'I Hate Myself and Want To Die' on *The Beavis and Butthead Experience*, and 'Moist Vagina,'

discretely renamed 'MV' on the 'All Apologies' single (which was not accompanied by a video). Cobain also appeared on a one-sided single released by T/K Records, *The 'Priest' They Called Him*, playing guitar behind William Burroughs as the legendary beat writer read a short story.

Nirvana also played two notable gigs during the tour, both for MTV. On November 18, they taped an appearance on MTV Unplugged, a truly magical performance that revealed the strength of the band's songs. On December 13, they headlined MTV's Live and Loud show, taped for broadcast on New Year's Eve. The band turned in a strong performance, and during the end-of-show destruction, a camera again caught the disturbing sight of Cobain spitting directly into the lens.

After a break for the holidays, the band would play a few more shows, and then begin what was expected to be a triumphant return to Europe in 1994.

BELOW: Nirvana victorious at the 1993 MTV Video Music Awards, on September 2, 1993. 'In Bloom' won Best Alternative Video; at right is the video's director, Kevin Kerslake.

Rape me
School
Breed
Sliver
Come as you are
Scentless apprentice
milk it
About A Girl
Lithium
Polly
Francis Farmer
Serve the Servants
Aneurysm
Teen Spurt
Territorial Pissings
Blew
all apologies
Heart Shaped box

LEFT: A handwritten setlist from 1993. Kurt's handwriting is easy to spot.

THE NIRVANA FAN CLUB

MAIL: P.O. BOX 5239
SHIP: 321 NEWARK ST. 5TH FLR
HOBOKEN, N.J. 07030

Dear _____ ,

It's time to change your name to **LUCKY!** You have been chosen from among
about a billion Nirvana fans in the Seattle area to attend the
**M T V   N I R V A N A
N E W   Y E A R S   E V E**
taping on
DECEMBER 13 , 1 9 9 3   5 : 0 0 P M
The taping will be held at
PIER 48 PORT OF SEATTLE
located at
101 ALASKA WAY SOUTH
in beautiful
SEATTLE, WASHINGTON

THIS IS NO JOKE !!!

Here's the scoop. You must arrive at the pier promptly at **4:00 PM.**
But, before you do anything, you must
**R S V P
201-420-8223**
by
DECEMBER 12, 1993

**THERE WILL BE NO ADMITTANCE AFTER
5:00 PM AND YOU MUST BRING THIS LETTER !!**

Congratulations and enjoy the show.

Love,

The Nirvana Fan Club
Gold Mountain Management
M T V
and
NIRVANA

LEFT: A few hundred lucky Nirvana fan club members received letters like this in December 1993. The concert took place on a pier in the harbour in downtown Seattle.

ABOVE: A rare, unused ticket to see Nirvana play the Bosnian Rape Victims Benefit concert of 1993.

IN UTERO

Nirvana's third album was their most self-conscious record. With *Bleach* they had simply wanted to be heard. With *Nevermind* they wanted to attract more attention than they'd been able to on an indie label. But now that the band was firmly in the spotlight, their every move being tracked, their next record was not just another release but the most anticipated album of the year. What would hottest band on the planet choose to do next?

In Nirvana's case, they chose to throw something of a curve ball, a record that lacked the commercial sheen of *Nevermind* and harkened back to their unvarnished punk rock roots. But the band were undeniably stronger musicians than they'd been when they began and Cobain's songwriting skills had developed as well, meaning Nirvana couldn't simply drop back into the lo-fi realm from which they'd come. Like it or not, the band's musical prowess had become more sophisticated. But *In Utero* was a more accurate depiction of the power of Nirvana's live show than any other album. Alternately abrasive and melodic, it

captured a band with the desire to push for musical extremes and with the capability – and the confidence – to pull it off.

Five of the album's songs had been knocking around since 1990 and '91; the opening riff of 'Rape Me' was even a reworking of the same riff that opened 'Smells Like Teen Spirit.' The band actually considered opening *In Utero* with the song, which would have more clearly made the album a direct response to *Nevermind* (which had opened with 'Teen Spirit'). But in the end they opted for a newer track to open the album, the no less pointed 'Serve The Servants,' whose lyrics commented on the band's (or more accurately, Cobain's) experience in the spotlight; though success might have "paid off well," it left the band surrounded by "self-appointed judges"; Cobain further dismissed his parents' "legendary" divorce as "such a bore."

Though Cobain denied there was much autobiographical element to the songs, *In Utero* has obvious references to his recent experiences. 'Rape Me' had been written before *Nevermind*'s success, but by *In Utero* Cobain had added a bridge that attacked the media and their "inside sources" that had plagued him. 'Frances Farmer Will Have Her Revenge On Seattle' referred to the Seattle actress Cobain felt a kinship with, due to her unconventional behavior, which led to her being institutionalized. A 'Radio Friendly Unit Shifter' is a cynical description of a commercially successful release; Cobain makes the prospect of producing such a work sound decidedly stressful, wedding the lyrics to a pile-driving beat while opening wondering what exactly is wrong with him.

In Utero contains some of Nirvana's harshest music. 'Milk It' starts out quietly, but regularly explodes into heavy riffing to match the dark lyrics. 'Tourette's' is a one-and-a-half minute thrash-fest, the kind of out and out rant you won't find on any other Nirvana release. 'Scentless Apprentice' (inspired by Patrick Süskind's novel *Perfume: The Story of a Murderer*) has exceptionally fierce music and the most frightening screams Cobain ever committed to record.

But there are also songs of poignant beauty. Both 'Dumb' and 'Pennyroyal Tea' evince an almost overwhelming world-weariness, sung from the perspective of someone who's both

FAR LEFT: A backstage pass for the 1993 *In Utero* tour.

ABOVE: Kurt during the 1993 *In Utero* tour, Nirvana's first – and only – arena tour.

LEFT: A crew-issue backstage pass for the band's *In Utero* tour of 1993.

physically and spiritually bereft. Both songs also have a strong sense of passivity that can be found elsewhere on the album, the sign of a soul in retreat, such as in the more aggressive 'Very Ape,' which has Cobain seemingly delighting in his own ignorance.

Cobain also freely mocks himself in the album's standout track, 'Heart-Shaped Box.' In *Nevermind*'s upbeat 'On A Plain,' he breezily sings that he can't complain, an admission quite at odds with his public image as a (in his words) "pissy, complaining, freaked-out schizophrenic." Conversely, as the chorus of 'Heart-Shaped Box' rushes in, he sends up his own image by gleefully reporting he has a new complaint. Phrases such as "magnet tar pit trap," "meat-eating orchids," and "umbilical noose" provide the most potent imagery in any Nirvana song, imagery that also suggests a profound ambivalence about relationships.

The concluding track, 'All Apologies,' has an insinuating, hypnotic melody that neatly masks the downhearted spirits of the lyric; steeped in guilt, Cobain is left wishing he could join the ranks of "easily amused" but lacking the motivation to do so, is instead left with nothing to do, nothing to say, nothing to write, an emptiness that led more than one critic to later observe the song seemed more like a suicide note. Cobain, of course, would insist he was merely being sarcastic. And as on *Nevermind*, it wasn't quite the end; after 24 minutes of silence came another "hidden" track, 'Gallons of Rubbing Alcohol Flow Through The Strip,' that rambled on for nearly 10 minutes. Contradictory to the end, Nirvana – and Cobain — always wanted to leave you guessing what was going to happen next.

RIGHT: Kurt playing one of his final Seattle shows, December 13, 1993. The show was taped for MTV's *Live and Loud* New Year's Eve special.

BELOW: Steve Albini was brought in as Producer for the band's third studio album. He is pictured here on stage with his band Shellac.

To the outside world, it seemed as if all was well in the Nirvana camp. *In Utero* had been well received, as had the Unplugged performance (which first aired in December). The *In Utero* tour had been going smoothly, and there was talk that Nirvana would be headlining the Lollapalooza festival in the summer of 1994. Michael Azerrad's *Come As You Are: The Story of Nirvana*, written with the band's cooperation and published in October 1993 to coincide with the tour, noted that having weathered the controversies of the past few years, band morale was now "at an all-time high."

> " **The worst crime I can think of would be to rip people off by faking it and pretending as if I'm having 100 percent fun.** "
>
> Kurt Cobain

But behind the scenes, it was a different story. In 1993, Cobain had fallen back into heroin addiction, and began using so excessively he had numerous overdoses. He OD'd before the New Music Seminar show the previous July, and Charles Cross' *Heavier Than Heaven* stated that Cobain had "as many as a dozen" overdoses during the year. An intervention held in June '93 had failed; during the tour break in December, Cobain had once again attempted a "hotel detox" while staying at the Canyon Ranch Spa in Tucson, Arizona. But he was soon back on drugs, and not looking forward to the upcoming European tour.

In early January, Nirvana played a few shows in Washington and Vancouver, B.C.; their final shows were January 7 and 8 at the Seattle Center Arena. The European tour wouldn't start until February, and during the break Cobain and Love moved into a new home, a mansion in Seattle's tony Madrona district, overlooking Lake Washington. At the end of the month, a session was arranged at a studio in the Seattle suburb of Shoreline, Robert Lang Studios, which was near Grohl's home.

But Cobain didn't turn up for the first two days of the session (which was produced by Adam Kaspar, who would go on to work with Grohl's Foo Fighters), January 28 and 29, leaving Novoselic and Grohl to work on their own. When Cobain finally arrived on the third day, the band worked on a song they'd been practicing at soundchecks and had played at a show on October 23 in Chicago. The band recorded the song, then known as "Kurt's Tune #1", quickly, and after a dinner break, Cobain recorded his vocal. It was the last recording session Nirvana would do.

Nirvana's European tour began on February 4 with an appearance on the French TV show *Nulle Part Ailleurs*. The musicians wore identical outfits; black trousers, vests, and ties, and white shirts, a look Cobain called their "Knack outfits." The band performed 'Rape Me,' 'Pennyroyal Tea,' and 'Drain You,' during which Cobain's guitar started to malfunction, causing him to drop it and finish the song screaming into the mic. But as the tour progressed, Cobain became increasingly ill. In addition to his sore throat and stomach problems, he was relying on tranquilizers when he couldn't get access to heroin, and he became increasingly tired and depressed. The change in his demeanor was obvious in the band's appearance on the Italian show *Tunnel*, when they performed 'Serve The Servants' and 'Dumb.' While Novoselic and Smear bounce around with good humor, Cobain remains oblivious.

He spoke openly about wanting to cancel the rest of the tour.

On March 1, Nirvana played what was to be the first of two dates in Munich. Before the show, Cobain had got in an argument with his wife over the phone, afterwards stating he wanted a divorce and to break up Nirvana. The show went on as scheduled, though there was a momentary disruption when the power went out. After the show (the last song performed was 'Heart-Shaped Box') Cobain told the band's booking agent he wanted the next night cancelled.

ABOVE: This photograph is from one of Kurt's final live appearances in the USA. It was snapped in late 1993 or 1994.

RIGHT: Proposed cover for the withdrawn 'Pennyroyal Tea' single.

OPPOSITE: Kurt on stage with Fender guitar in Italy, at the Modena Palasport on February 21, 1994.

A short break was coming up anyway, and Cobain and Smear flew to Rome on March 2. Love arrived the following day, having been busy promoting her upcoming album with Hole, *Live Through This*, in England.

That night, Cobain drank champagne and had taken a number of Rohypnol pills, a medication used for insomnia. Cobain was rushed to the hospital the next morning, and he remained in a coma for 20 hours.

While the event was publicly described as an accident, Love had found what appeared to be a suicide note in her husband's hand. But a number of those close to Cobain weren't told the incident was a suicide attempt. Cobain and Love flew back to Seattle on March 12. Nirvana's European dates had been rescheduled, and it was still hoped the band would play Lollapalooza. But Cobain was no longer interested, and when Love forbade him to do drugs in their home, he simply went elsewhere to use them.

In desperation, Love set up another invention on March 25, during which she told Cobain she was going to LA to try and undergo detox herself, asking Cobain to accompany her. He refused. Love left for LA the same day, and Cobain finally agreed

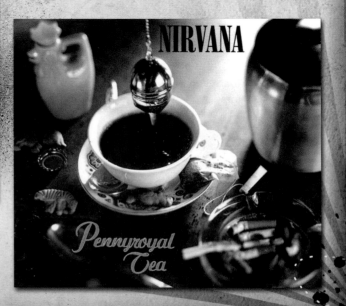

NIRVANA

Pennyroyal Tea

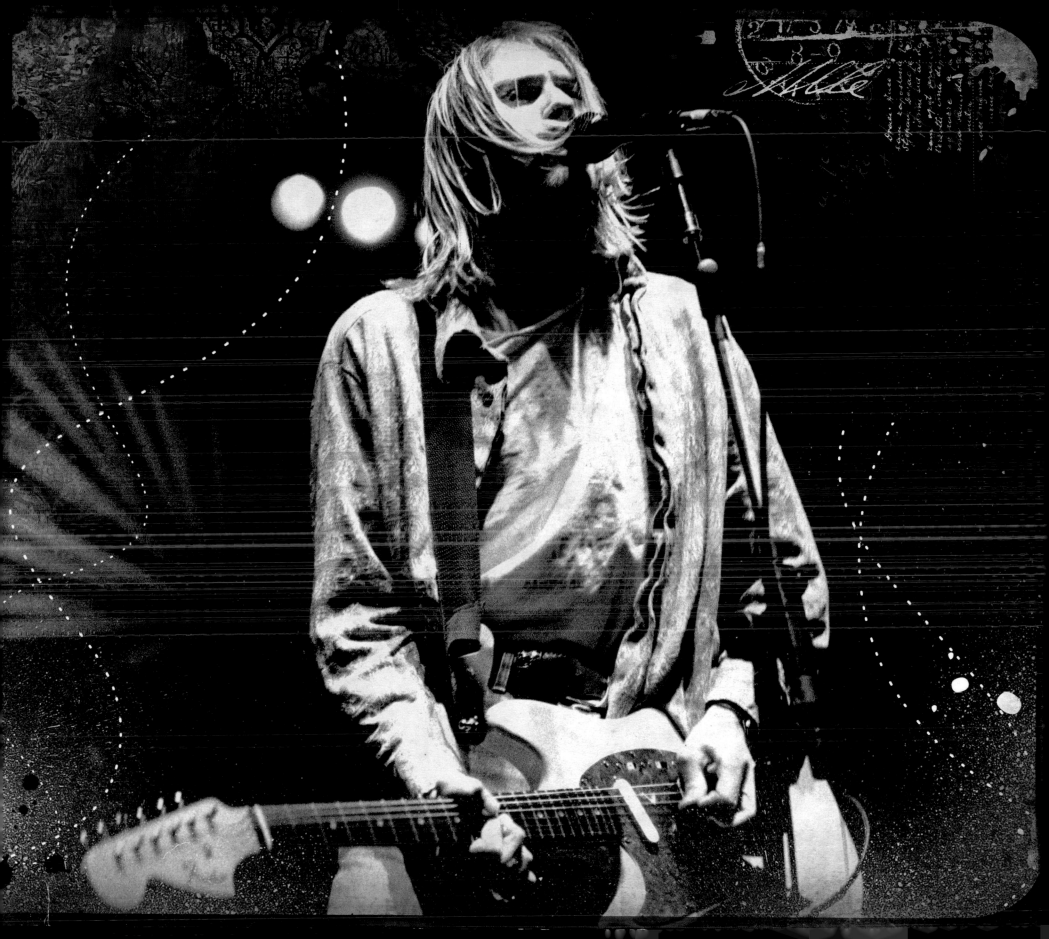

to fly down on March 29. Novoselic drove him to the airport, but Cobain ran off after getting in a fight with him at the terminal. But the next day, Cobain again agreed to try rehab, and flew to LA, checking in at the Exodus Recovery Center.

During his brief stay, Frances was brought to see him, and Cobain also spoke with Love (who was at the Peninsula Beverly Hills, going through another "hotel detox") over the phone. But on the evening of April 1, he left Exodus by climbing over a back wall, and then flew back to Seattle.

On the morning of April 2, he went to a sporting goods store and bought a box of shotgun shells; he'd purchased a new shotgun hours before leaving for Exodus on March 30. There were scattered sightings of him over the next few days. Love also cancelled Cobain's credit cards, hoping to restrict his movements, and hired a private detective; the stress led to her checking into Exodus later that week. But despite all the searching, Cobain couldn't be found.

On Friday, April 8, an electrician arrived at Cobain's home to install an alarm system. Looking through a window at a room above the garage, he spotted what he first thought was a mannequin and then realized was a body. The police were summoned, and the body was identified as Cobain's, dead from a self-inflicted shotgun wound to the head; it was later determined the date of death was probably April 5. A suicide note was found, addressed to Cobain's imaginary childhood friend, "Boddah." The note revealed a man in emotional turmoil, whose lack of interest in creating music made him feel "guilty": "The worst crime I can think of would be to rip people off by faking it and pretending as if I'm having 100 percent fun." His feelings for people were also conflicted, at one point stating, "Since the age of seven I've become hateful towards all humans in general," but elsewhere admitting, "I love and feel for people too much." The note was signed "Peace, love, empathy, Kurt Cobain." After a few lines addressed to Love, Cobain ended the note with a simple "I love you. I love you!"

News of Cobain's death spread quickly. Love immediately returned to Seattle. Both Nirvana's record label and management issued statements, but Novoselic and Grohl were unavailable for comment. Sub Pop Records had an anniversary party scheduled for April 9; they considered canceling, but eventually decided against it, and the evening became an unofficial wake for the music community. A public vigil, organized by Seattle radio stations KNDD, KISW, and KXRX, was held on April 10, at the Seattle Center's Flag Plaza. There were short speeches from a local minister, a representative from the Crisis Clinic, and a poet. A DJ also read a letter from Larry Smith, one of Cobain's uncles by marriage.

Taped statements from Novoselic and Love were also played. Novoselic's was low-key, stressing the egalitarian aspect of making music: "If you've got a guitar and a lot of soul, just bang something out and mean it. You're the superstar, plugged into the tones and rhythms that are uniquely and universally human: music." Love's statement was much more fraught. She read most of Cobain's suicide note, interjecting her own comments ("No, Kurt, the worst crime I can think of is for you to just continue being a rock star when you fuckin' hated it."). Afterwards, as Nirvana's music played over the speakers, attendees climbed into a fountain behind the Plaza, lingering on in defiance even after the music had been turned off.

Not far away, a private service was being held at the Unity Church of Truth. Mourners were given a program that featured a picture of Cobain as a child; guitar tech Earnie Bailey put together a tape that had some of Cobain's favorite songs by the Beatles and the Vaselines. After the service was over, Love went to the Seattle Center; the public vigil had ended, but she spoke with fans that remained, passing out items of Cobain's clothing and showing people his suicide note.

Cobain's death marked the first time a major rock star had committed suicide, and there was much attendant publicity. Nirvana's career, which had exploded into the mainstream with such unexpected ferocity a mere two and a half years before, was now over. It was a great loss to the world of music. But it was saddest of all for those closest to Cobain, who had now lost a man who was a son, a father, a husband, and a friend.

LEFT and ABOVE: Kurt in pyjamas, in one of the final photo shoots that he posed for in 1994. By April of that year he was dead.

OPPOSITE: One of the band's last concerts in the USA. Few people in the crowd were to suspect that this would be the last ever time Kurt played on American shores.

LEFT: A rare poster advertising Nirvana's concert in Barcelona, Spain in February of 1994. It was to be the last time they ever played that country.

ABOVE: A ticket for Nirvana's concert in Brixton, London in April of 1994. It was one of many concerts that the band never played.

OPPOSITE: A section from the official tour itinerary for what was to be the band's final tour. Their final concert was in Germany on March 1, 1994.

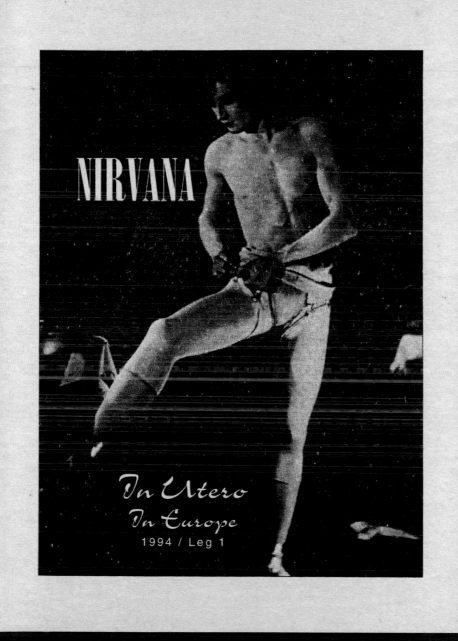

NIRVANA

In Utero
In Europe
1994 / Leg 1

NIRVANA
February 1994

MONDAY	TUESDAY	WEDNESDAY	THURSDAY	FRIDAY	SATURDAY	SUNDAY
	Crew in England for pre-production **1**	Band departs USA **2**	Band flies London to Paris / Crew flies to Lisbon **3**	Band / Paris television taping **4**	Band flies Paris to Lisbon **5**	LISBON, PORTUGAL / Pavilhao D. Cascais **6**
MADRID, SPAIN / Day Off **7**	MADRID, SPAIN / Real Madrid **8**	BARCELONA, SPAIN / Palalo desportes **9**	TOULOUSE, FRANCE / Palais des Sport **10**	TOULON, FRANCE / Day Off **11**	TOULON, FRANCE / Zenith **12**	PARIS, FRANCE / Day Off **13**
PARIS, FRANCE / Zenith **14**	PARIS / FRANCE / Zenith / Salle Omnisports **15**	RENNES, FRANCE / Omnisports **16**	GRENOBLE, FRANCE / Day Off **17**	GRENOBLE, FRANCE / Le Summum **18**	NEUCHATEL, SWITZERLAND / Patinoires Littoral **19**	MODENA, ITALY / Day Off **20**
MODENA, ITALY / Palasport **21**	TURIN, ITALY / Palaghiaccio **22**	MILAN, ITALY / Day Off **23**	MILAN, ITALY / Palatrussardi **24**	MILAN, ITALY / Palatrussardi **25**	LJUBLJANA SLOVENIA / Day Off **26**	LJUBLJANA SLOVENIA / Hala Tivoli **27**
MUNICH, GERMANY / Day Off **28**						

NIRVANA
March 1994

MONDAY	TUESDAY	WEDNESDAY	THURSDAY	FRIDAY	SATURDAY	SUNDAY
	MUNICH, GERMANY / Terminal 1 **1**	MUNICH, GERMANY / Terminal 1 **2**	OFFENBACH, GERMANY / Stadthalle **3**	End of Leg 1 / Europe **4**	Off **5**	Off **6**
Off **7**	Off **8**	Off **9**	Off **10**	Begin Leg 2 – Europe '94 / PRAGUE, CZECH. REPUBLIC **11**	Europe '94 **12**	**13**
14	**15**	**16**	**17**	**18**	**19**	**20**
21	**22**	**23**	**24**	**25**	**26**	**27**
28	**29**	**30**	**31**			

NIRVANA

PERSONNEL LIST

KURT COBAIN
KRIST NOVOSELIC
DAVE GROHL
PAT SMEAR
MELORA CREAGER

BAND CREW
ALEX MACLEOD
JEFF MASON
KELLY NASH
SUSANNE BASIC
CRAIG OVERBAY
IAN BEVERIDGE
JIM VINCENT
GARRY MACKENZIE
JOHN DUNCAN
ED SWINK
PETER CURRIER
ALBERT THORG

SOUND CREW
ALLAN BAGLEY (PROSHOW)
NIKO VONK (PRO SHOW)
JOHN EVANS (SSE)

LIGHTING CREW
MIKE LAMB (LSD)
PAT CONNOLLY (LSD)
GARY VASPOL (LSD)

CATERING CREW
LISA GIBBLEY
MICHAEL THORNTON
PETER BAILEY
SUZANNE DEXTER
NUALA KEEGAN

BUS DRIVERS
CHRIS MOYNIHAN
JOHN CURTIS
IAN HUNTER
NOEL KERSHAW

TRUCK DRIVERS
MARTIN PALMER
FRASER AITKEN
PETER COOK
KEVIN BARNES

DATE: TUESDAY, MARCH 1
CITY: MUNICH, GERMANY
VENUE: TERMINAL 1

TRAVEL: NONE

HOTELS:
BAND: BAYERISCHER HOF
PROMENADEPLATZ 6
8000 MUNICH 22, GERMANY
PHONE: (49-89) 212-00
FAX: (49-89) 212-0906
CHECK OUT: PM ON 2ND
TO VENUE: 20 MINUTES
TO AIRPORT: 65 MINUTES
ROOM SERV: 24 HOURS
TO CITY CTR: 10 MINUTES
RESTAURANT: ISAR TERRASSEN (BUFFET) 6:30-11:30 AM; 12-3:00 PM; 6:03 PM-1:00 AM; HILTON GRILL 12 NOON-9:00 PM; 9:00-11:00 PM
TV: FULL CABLE, CNN, MTV, EUROSPORT, JAPANESE CHANNEL AND IN-HOUSE MOVIES (PPV)
ACTIVITIES: BEACH CLUB WITH INDOOR POOL, SAUNA, MASSAGE AND STEAM BATH

CREW: MARRIOTT
BERLINER STRASSE 93
D-80805 MUNICH, GERMANY
PHONE: (49-89) 360-020
FAX: (49-89) 360-02200
CHECK OUT: AM ON 2ND

PRODUCTION:
TERMINAL 1
ADDRESS: AIRPORT - MUNCHEN - RIEHM
MUNICH, GERMANY
CAPACITY: 3050
LOAD IN: 9:00 AM
MAIN PHONE: (49-89) 90-63-22

PROD. PHONE: (49-89) 90-70-75
PROD. FAX: (49-89) 90-81-55
DOORS: 6:30 PM

PROMOTER: MAREK LIEBERBERG
COMPANY: KONZERTAGENTUR GMBH
ADDRESS: MORIKESTRASSE 14
6000 FRANKFURT, GERMANY
PHONE / FAX: (49-69) 558-193 / 568-245

THE MELVINS
SHOWTIME: 8:00-8:45 PM

NIRVANA
SHOWTIME: 9:05 PM

BAND AFTER SHOW TRAVEL: NONE

CREW AFTER SHOW TRAVEL: NONE

NOTES:

MTV UNPLUGGED

When the audience entered Sony Music Studios on W 54th Street in New York City on the evening of November 18, 1993 for Nirvana's appearance on MTV's *Unplugged* show, they came into a room bathed in an orange, autumnal glow. Thick velvet curtains were draped on the walls, a chandelier hung from the ceiling, and lilies and candles decorated the stage. A strong atmospheric presence had been set before a single note had even been played.

Those who were present felt a noticeable sense of anticipation about what was to come. Part of it was the thrill of seeing Nirvana, but there was also a touch of apprehension; how could a band known for wreaking as much havoc on stage as Nirvana possibly tone themselves down to fit into the *Unplugged* format?

We should have known better. Nirvana pulled it off majestically, turning in the kind of heartfelt performance that sent shivers up your spine. But by the time the album came out, in November 1994, it had taken on a new meaning. Instead of being Nirvana's first official live album, it was now a tribute record, the first album released in

the wake of Cobain's death. Which is something that's colored the perception of Nirvana's *Unplugged* appearance ever since.

But in that brief period between when the show first aired in December 1993 and Cobain's death in April 1994, *Unplugged* revealed what the fans already knew, and more casual listeners hadn't yet realized; beneath the fuzzy guitars, pounding bass and thundering drums, Nirvana's songs were exceptionally well crafted. This performance also revealed more of the band's influences than usual, including an unprecedented six covers – nearly half of the set list. There was some broadening of the band's musical palette as well; in addition to second guitarist Pat Smear, cellist Lori Goldston, from Seattle's Black Cat Orchestra, provided somber accompaniment, and Novoselic unexpectedly demonstrated his skill on the accordion.

The band's musicianship is flawless throughout; unlike other *Unplugged* shows, which required numerous retakes, Nirvana simply played through their set like they would at any other show. But it's Cobain's voice that makes the greatest impression. Suddenly exposed as a singer in a way he'd never experienced before, with

no wall of sound to hide behind, his voice has an emotive, plaintive quality that's a key reason why the show has become one of Nirvana's most memorable performances.

The band eases into the "unplugged" setting by opening with 'About A Girl,' an obvious contender being acoustically driven to begin with. The same can be said of 'Come As You Are,' 'Polly,' 'Something In The Way,' and 'Dumb.' But in every song, there's something that's different from the studio versions. Cobain's voice has an edge, a keenness, that's more subdued on the records. The underlying melancholy is also enhanced; whereas 'Come As You Are' sounded fairly relaxed and laid back on *Nevermind*, on *Unplugged* there's a slight catch of desperation as he reaches for the top notes. One would hardly think Cobain could sound any more despairing in 'Something In The Way' than he does on *Nevermind*, but that's exactly what happens here. When he falters on 'Pennyroyal Tea,' nearly coming in on the wrong note, it's a moment that makes the song even more heartbreaking. 'On A Plain,' an unusual choice to begin with, loses the optimistic tinge it had on *Nevermind*, and becomes almost sorrowful.

The cover song choices further enhance the downbeat mood (it was later noted that a number of the songs also reference death). One of the most striking is David Bowie's 'The Man Who Sold The World.' It was the first time the band had performed the song, and Cobain stumbles over the guitar line, a deeply affecting performance, no one then suspecting that the line about the man "who died alone" would be even more haunting in just a few months time. Nirvana regularly covered the Vaselines, but in contrast to their other covers, their take on the Scottish duo's 'Jesus Doesn't Want Me For A Sunbeam' is decidedly subdued, with the addition of Novoselic's accordion a nice, and unexpected, touch. MTV might have been unhappy with the Meat Puppets' guest appearance (they

were hoping for Pearl Jam), but their inclusion was truer to Nirvana's alternative credentials.

'All Apologies' could have provided a fine concluding note for the evening. But Nirvana had something else in mind. Cobain and Novoselic had played on Mark Lanegan's version of the folk ballad 'Where Did You Sleep Last Night' which had appeared on Lanegan's *The Winding Sheet* album, and the song occasionally appeared in Nirvana's set lists. But on this occasion, the band went all out, with Cobain delivering a stunning, even frightening, vocal performance, such was the intensity. It was the perfect conclusion to a remarkable evening, one that would open up Nirvana's talents to a wider audience.

ABOVE and OPPOSITE: Though Kurt joked during the show that Nirvana was a "rich rock band," he nonetheless had to make do with a guitar designed for a right-handed player, as revealed by the position of the guitar's scratch plate.

WISHKAH

Initially planned for release in 1994, this live album didn't appear until 1996, when Novoselic and Grohl finally felt emotionally ready to sift through hours of tapes and compile the definitive Nirvana concert experience. For the album's title, they returned to Cobain's and Novoselic's home town; the Wishkah is one of two rivers running through Aberdeen.

Surprisingly, despite the songs being drawn from ten different performances over five years (from a December 3, 1989 show in London to a January 7, 1994 show in Seattle – both misdated in the album's liner notes), the record hangs together very well. At 54 minutes, it's about the length of one of Nirvana's club shows, and even kicks off as a number of 1989 shows did – Cobain screaming at full volume before the band launches into the opening riff of 'School.' The set list focuses on the more upbeat (and, especially in the case of 'Tourette's,' more punishing) numbers; aside from a nod to the band's softer side on 'Polly,' you won't find any 'Come As You Are,' 'Dumb,' or 'Pennyroyal Tea.' It could be, of course, an effort to vary the song mix of officially released live tracks, given that those three songs previously appeared on *Unplugged*. But it also points directly to Nirvana's biggest strength – the galvanizing power of their live performances.

Nirvana, after all, first made their reputation as a live act; three, or sometimes four, musicians who at their best fully gave themselves over to the music in a release of joyous, unbridled passion. The band had played live for two and a half years before releasing their first album, repeatedly honing their craft as they rose from hopeful amateurs to confident professionals. And despite the controversies that dogged the band once *Nevermind* hit, their live shows revealed that they never lost the ability to be rejuvenated by the simple pleasure of making music together.

After the opening barrage of 'School,' from the band's November 25, 1991 performance at the Paradiso in Amsterdam, come three numbers from a December 28, 1991 show in Del Mar, California. Nine out of the record's 16 songs are from the band's 1991 fall shows, and as Novoselic points out in the album's liner notes, the band was "particularly aggressive" during the Del Mar show, widely regarded as one of Nirvana's best. Cobain's raspy voice on 'Drain You' reveals the strain of the band's non-stop touring, but also adds an edgy fierceness to a raging performance of 'Aneurysm.' Then comes The Hit – 'Smells Like Teen Spirit' that is – pounded out with an intense fury. One wonders if Cobain suspected even then how the rock star ride might turn out for him; in the song's chorus, it sounds as if he's changed "it's less dangerous," to "it is dangerous."

It's back to Amsterdam for a punchy 'Been A Son,' then 'Lithium,' which hasn't yet graduated to the audience singalong status it would achieve later, Cobain sounding almost giddy during the sustained "Yeahs!" in the chorus. 'Sliver,' from 1993, bumps up the tempo (Nirvana was never one of those bands that tried to replicate the studio version of a song in live performance), curtailing some of the nostalgic pull, but adding the kind of energy that comes from seeing a band perform live.

ABOVE and RIGHT Two shots of Kurt and Krist at Reading 1992. *Wishkah* featured one song from this appearance; the full performance would be officially released in 2009.

OPPOSITE: Underneath the bridge, by the Wishkah River in Aberdeen, Washington, one of Kurt's many hangouts, and the setting which inspired the song 'Something In The Way.' A commemorative sign was hung on the bridge's supports after the release of the *Wishkah* album.

Novoselic refers in the liner notes to 'Spank Thru' (from a '91 show) being "actually the first Nirvana song," so it's interesting have the song followed by two numbers from later in the band's career, 'Scentless Apprentice,' and 'Heart-Shaped Box,' both from 1993 shows, which clearly illustrate how Cobain's songwriting (and the band's musicianship) developed and progressed, from the novelty song approach of 'Spank Thru' to the complex and disturbing undercurrents unleashed in the latter two songs (with

'Scentless Apprentice' being the album's musical high point).

Ah, but there's nothing like a pure blast of noise, and 'Milk It' (from the band's penultimate US date, January 7, 1994) and 'Negative Creep' (from a Halloween '91 show) gloriously revel in their raging depictions of self-loathing. Coming near the end are 'Polly' and 'Breed,' from the final night of Nirvana's 1989 European tour; the schedule had been exhausting, and Cobain's reduced to skipping many of the words in 'Breed,' but

the band remains nonetheless determined to squeeze out every last remaining bit of energy. Finally, following the outburst of 'Tourette's,' comes 'Blew', the last song here as in so many other Nirvana shows. The first known live performance of the song was on March 19, 1988 in Tacoma, Washington; the last came six years later, March 1, 1994 in Munich, Germany. By which time Nirvana had risen from the muddy banks of the Wishkah to conquer the world.

WHAT HAPPENED NEXT

Nirvana was over. There would be no studio-crafted reunions, *a la* the Beatles with "Free As A Bird," no partial stage reunions bringing in the original band and a new lead singer, as The Doors and Alice in Chains have done. But Nirvana's story continued.

In the wake of Cobain's death, Nirvana's album sales surged. In the US, *In Utero* jumped from #72 to #27 in the charts, while *Incesticide* re-entered the charts at #47, and *Nevermind*, which was still in the Top 200 at #167, moved up to #56. But the record company was wary of being seen as cashing in on Cobain's death, and a planned single release of "Pennyroyal Tea" was scrapped (it didn't help that one of the B-sides was to be "I Hate Myself and Want to Die"). However, they did go ahead with the release of the compilation *DGC Rarities Vol. 1* in July, as it had been in the works long before Cobain died; it featured the Smart Studios version of "Pay To Play" (an early version of "Stay Away").

Novoselic and Grohl gave no interviews at the time. They made a surprise appearance with the Stinky Puffs (led by ten-year-old Simon Timony, then the stepson of Jad Fair from Half Japanese) on the opening night of Olympia alt-rock fest Yo Yo a Go Go on July 12. On September 8, Pat Smear joined them onstage at the MTV Music Video Awards, where "Heart-Shaped Box" won Best Alternative Video and Best Art Direction; Novoselic also introduced a short tribute film compiled by Dave Markey.

Novoselic and Grohl also spent the summer working on a double album set then called *Verse Chorus Verse*, which would feature an album of Nirvana's live tracks and the *Unplugged* show. But they found it too emotionally overwhelming to go through all the tapes,

BELOW: This star is embedded outside Rosevear's Music Store in Aberdeen, where Kurt and Krist each took guitar lessons.

RIGHT: Many fans who showed up for the Seattle vigil wore home-made shirts like this one, decorated with Nirvana song titles.

OPPOSITE: Nirvana fans congregate around the Seattle Center fountain on the day of Kurt Cobain's public vigil, April 10, 1994.

Kurt Cobain
Lead Singer
'Nirvana'

so the set was scaled back to the single album, *MTV Unplugged In New York*, released in November. It was accompanied a few weeks later by the feature-length video *Live! Tonight! Sold Out!!* a great document of live footage spanning Nirvana's career, including their infamous *Top of the Pops* appearance.

In 1995, Grohl formed Foo Fighters, who would go on to find incredible success. Novoselic formed his own bands, Sweet 75 and Eyes Adrift, and later played with a band that had been a key musical influence for him; Flipper. In 1996, the live album *From The Muddy Banks of the Wishkah* was released, entering the US charts at #1 and reaching #3 in the UK. Additional tracks trickled out on various compilations.

A box set of Nirvana rarities was originally planned for release in the fall of 2001 (the tenth anniversary release of *Nevermind*), but the release did not happen at that time. The following year, however, saw the release of the "best of" collection, *Nirvana*. The album featured the last song the band had worked on, in January 1994 at Robert Lang Studios, 'Kurt's Tune #1,' which was renamed 'You Know You're Right.' It was classic Nirvana, alternately brooding, powerful, and intense.

The long-awaited box set finally arrived in 2004. *With The Lights Out* featured rarities, previously unreleased tracks, and a bonus DVD. *Sliver: The Best of the Box*, released the following year, had three tracks that hadn't been on the box set, including the Fecal Matter version of "Spank Thru" — 20 years after the track had originally been recorded.

There since have been further releases. *Live! Tonight! Sold Out!!* and *Unplugged* have both been released on DVD with additional footage, and 2009 saw the release of *Live At Reading*, documenting Nirvana's 1992 appearance at the festival, on CD and DVD. New releases will undoubtedly follow in the future, perhaps covering the band's radio performances or other live shows.

Nirvana shook up the music industry at a time when the music scene felt stagnant. For a brief time, major label doors opened to other alternative acts — including the Melvins, Mudhoney and the Meat Puppets — most of whom were dropped when they didn't achieve Nirvana-like success. But Nirvana's influence remains, not only in their music, but also in their attitude. Their songs are rightly hailed as being rock 'n' roll classics. And, at their best, their shows had a joyous spirit of inclusion; not the separation of star performers and audience, but that of a community united in the love of music played with the utmost passion.

It's a welcoming spirit you can still find a trace of in Aberdeen. In 2004, the Kurt Cobain Memorial Committee was founded by local residents seeking a way to honor Cobain, and Nirvana. Their first endeavor was to modify the "Welcome to Aberdeen" sign that greets people arriving into town. The message on the smaller sign that hangs beneath the main one had to both connect with Nirvana fans and have a universal appeal for non-fans as well. The committee finally found a Nirvana song title that was perfect. It was welcoming, non-judgmental, and in a very real way expressed Nirvana's own open-minded attitude toward their music and their career: "Come As You Are".

LEFT: Dave and Krist are good friends who have collaborated on a few post-Nirvana projects.

RIGHT: A flyer advertising the *Live! Tonight! Sold Out!!* DVD release.

OPPOSITE: Dave with his fellow Foo Fighters.

THE HOME VIDEO

NIRVANA

LIVE! TONIGHT! SOLD OUT!!

Conceived by Kurt Cobain, Live! Tonight! Sold Out!! has come to fruition after three years in the making. A chronicle of the Nevermind days, the 83-minute home video features previously-unreleased footage of live performances during Nirvana's international tour, interviews, behind-the-scenes tomfoolery and shots from the band's own home video archives.

WITH THE LIGHTS OUT

Initially planned for release in 2001, as a tie-in with the tenth anniversary of *Nevermind*'s release, fans had to wait patiently another three years for this set. When *With The Lights Out* was finally released in 2004, it was clear a lot of effort had gone into its creation to make the box set something special. Instead of simply offering an overview of the band's career through officially released tracks (an approach used on numerous other sets), *With The Lights Out* was dominated by tracks that hadn't been released officially, with about a third previously unavailable to even the wiliest bootlegger.

And the set opens with just such a track, from Nirvana's very first show in March 1987 at a house party in Raymond, Washington. Their cover of Led Zeppelin's 'Heartbreaker' reveals the band's influences, but their own voice would start emerging soon enough. 'Mrs. Butterworth' is a fascinating example of Cobain's development as a songwriter, and a song that wouldn't emerge from rehearsal; though Cobain would use some of the lyrical ideas in 'Swap Meet,' the song was never known to have been performed live.

Even more historic is the first known recorded version of 'Smells Like Teen Spirit,' taped at a band rehearsal shortly before the band went to California to record *Nevermind*. Even with most of the lyrics not completed, and the musical arrangement not entirely nailed down (not to mention the sound being less than sterling, given that the song was recorded on a boom box), the power of the 'Teen Spirit' is evident. This is same version producer Butch Vig heard as he was preparing for the *Nevermind* sessions, and it's easy to see why this was the song he was most excited about.

And there are plenty of other nods to Cobain's songwriting process. There are solo demos of 'About A Girl,' 'Sliver,' 'Serve The Servants,' and one of the last songs he wrote, 'You Know You're Right.' Most haunting is another demo recorded shortly before his death, 'Do Re Mi,' a delicate, mournful number with an achingly bittersweet vocal. There's insight into the band's creative process as well, heard to most exciting effect on a rehearsal of 'Scentless Apprentice,' where you actually hear the song coming together. *Nevermind* is such a classic album it's hard to imagine which songs one would choose to leave off, but here you're offered examples of two songs that might have made the cut, 'Verse Chorus Verse' and 'Old Age,' mellower songs the band rarely played again after this session.

The set's tracks that had been released were songs that had appeared as B-sides ('Curmudgeon') or were on compilations that were now out of print (a cover of the Velvet Underground's 'Here She Comes Now'). There were also some nice surprises, most welcome being 'Ain't It A Shame,' from a 1989 session when Cobain and Novoselic worked with Screaming Trees' Mark Lanegan and Mark Pickerel; a lovely rehearsal version of 'Jesus Don't Wants Me For A Sunbeam' from 1994 shows that whatever personal problems surrounded the band, their musical work together remained harmonious.

The three CDs were supplemented by a DVD that was just as revelatory, especially considering that all but three numbers are pre-*Nevermind* (in contrast, all the songs from the *Live! Tonight! Sold Out!!* DVD are post-*Nevermind*). The first nine numbers show how humble the group's beginnings were; it's a rehearsal in Novoselic's mother's home, with their friends hanging out, and a (filmed) break taken to buy a case of beer. Linking sequences show the band touring rough, hauling out mattresses from their battered van to bed down for the night. There's footage of Grohl's first show with the band on a cramped stage, as well as the first public performance of 'Teen Spirit' at Seattle's OK Hotel. It was all the years of hard work that helped make the band such a compelling live act; the performance of 'Jesus Don't Want Me For A Sunbeam' from a Seattle show in 1991 shows the band to be fully confident performers, having made the transition from clubs to theatres with ease. The DVD closes with footage of the band stumbling through a performance of 'Seasons in the Sun' while the band was in Brazil. Though the performance is rough, it's undeniably heartbreaking, considering both the song's theme (a young man facing an early death) and the fact that it was the first single Cobain said he ever bought.

The single disc *Sliver: The Best of the Box* followed in 2005, with three additional tracks, including the first ever release of a song from the Fecal Matter tape, 'Spank Thru.' Together, the two recordings spanned nine years, capturing every phase of Nirvana's career, revealing that far from being slackers, Nirvana remained a band determinedly committed to their music.

ABOVE RIGHT: Here We Are, Now Entertain Us: One of *With The Lights Out*'s most interesting tracks is the first known recorded version of 'Smells Like Teen Spirit'.

RIGHT: Pre-CD Days: Nirvana promotional cassettes.

OPPOSITE: Nirvana in New York City, July 24, 1993. The band that changed the face of alternative rock left behind a potent musical legacy that's still enthralling.

SELECTED DISCOGRAPHY

NIRVANA ALBUMS

1989 *Bleach* (Sub Pop)

1991 *Nevermind* (DGC)

1992 *Incesticide* (DGC)

1993 *In Utero* (DGC)

1994 *Unplugged In New York* (DGC)

1996 *From The Muddy Banks Of The Wishkah* (DGC)

2009 *Live At Reading* (Geffen)

NIRVANA COLLECTIONS

2002 *Nirvana* (DGC)

2004 *With The Lights Out* (DGC)

2005 *Sliver: The Best Of The Box* (Geffen)

2010 *Icon* (Geffen)

2011 *Nevermind: The Singles* (Universal)

NIRVANA ON COMPILATIONS

1988 *Sub Pop 200* (Sub Pop) 'Spank Thru'

1989 *Teriyaki Asthma Vol. 1* (EP; C/Z) 'Mexican Seafood'

1990 *Hard To Believe* (C/Z) 'Do You Love Me?'
Heaven And Hell (Imaginary) 'Here She Comes Now'

1991 *Teriyaki Asthma Vols. I-IV* (album; C/Z) 'Mexican Seafood'
Kill Rock Stars (Kill Rock Stars) 'Beeswax'

1993 *Eight Songs For Greg Sage And The Wipers* (Tim Kerr) 'Return Of The Rat'

Fourteen Songs For Greg Sage And The Wipers
(album; Tim Kerr) 'Return Of The Rat'

No Alternative (Arista) 'Sappy'

The Beavis And Butthead Experience (DGC)
'I Hate Myself And I Want To Die'

1994 *DGC Rarities Vol. 1* (DGC) 'Pay To Play'

1996 *Home Alive: The Art Of Self Defense* (Epic)
'Radio Friendly Unit Shifter' (live)

SNL 25: The Musical Performances Vol. 2
(Dreamworks) 'Rape Me' (live)

NIRVANA SINGLES/EPS

1988 'Love Buzz'

1989 'Blew'

1990 'Sliver'

1991 'Molly's Lips' (split single with The Fluid)

'Here She Comes Now' (split single with Melvins)

'Smells Like Teen Spirit'

1992 'Come As You Are'

'Hormoaning' (EP)

'Lithium'

'In Bloom'

1993 'Oh The Guilt' (split single with Jesus Lizard)

'Heart-Shaped Box'

'All Apologies'

1994 'About A Girl' (live from Unplugged)

DAVE GROHL ALBUMS

As Pocketwatch:
1992 *Pocketwatch* (Simple Machines)

Dave Grohl solo:
1997 *Music From The Motion Picture* Touch
(Roswell/Capitol)

As Probot:
2004 *Probot* (Roswell/Southern Lord)

As Them Crooked Vultures:
2009 *Them Crooked Vultures* (DGC/Interscope)

As Foo Fighters:
1995 *Foo Fighters* (Roswell/Capitol)

1997 *The Colour And The Shape* (Roswell/Capitol)

1999 *There Is Nothing Left To Lose* (Roswell/Capitol)

2002 *One By One* (Roswell/RCA)

2005 *In Your Honor* (Roswell/RCA)

2006 *Skin And Bones* (Roswell/RCA)

2007 *Echoes, Silence, Patience & Grace* (Roswell/RCA)

2009 *Greatest Hits* (Roswell/RCA)

2011 *Wasting Light* (Roswell/RCA)

2011 *Medium Rare* (Roswell/RCA)

2014 *Sonic Highways* (Roswell/RCA)

Prior to joining Nirvana, Grohl was a member of Washington, DC-based bands Mission Impossible, Dain Bramage, and Scream, all of whom released recordings. He has also appeared as a guest musician on numerous other releases.

KRIST NOVOSELIC ALBUMS

As Sweet 75:
1997 *Sweet 75* (DGC)

As WTO Combo:
2000 *Live From The Battle In Seattle* (Alternative Tentacles)

As Eyes Adrift:
2002 *Eyes Adrift* (spinART)

As Flipper
2009 *Love* (MVD Audio)
2009 *Fight* (MVD Audio)

Novoselic has also appeared as a guest musician on various releases.

The publishers would like to thank the following sources for their kind permission to reproduce the pictures in this book.

Key: t = top, b = bottom, c = centre, l = left and r = right

© David "The Ack" Ackerman: 18r-19

Author's collection: 6-7, 10, 56, 87, 88l

Corbis: Bozi: 8r; /Matthias Clamer/Outline: 36b; /Henry Diltz: 74; / Marcel Noecker/dpa: 16t; /Charles Peterson/Retna Ltd: 38, 60c, 62, 70; /John Van Hasselt/Sygma: 89; /Niels Van Iperen/Retna Ltd.: 44bl

Getty Images: 90l; /Redferns: 37tc, 37tr; /Paul Bergen/Redferns: 56-57; /Raffaella Cavalieri/Redferns: 77; /David Corio/Redferns: 9; /Ian Dickson/Redferns: 39l; /Mick Hutson/Redferns: 86c, 86r; /Fotos International: 71; /Jeff Kravitz/FilmMagic: 61; /Michel Linssen/Redferns: 65l, 65r, 66; /Hayley Madden/Redferns: 47l; / Kevin Mazur/WireImage: 75r; /Frank Micelotta: 82, 83, 85; /Peter Pakvis/Redferns: 15; /Martin Philbey/Redferns: 37; /John Shearer/ WireImage: 36t; /Steve Pyke: 1, 58-59; /Time & Life Pictures: 60r; / Chris Walter/WireImage: 8l

Press Association Images: /Starfile: 48

Photoshot/Retna UK: 10, 13, 25, 27, 30-31, 32, 34, 46r, 54l, 54r, 55, 76c, 78l, 78r; /AJ Barratt: 40; /Bellia Dalle: 41; /Steve Double: 28, 84; /Martyn Goodacre: 4-5, 17, 96; /David Henderson/ Headpress: 58; /Charlie Hoselton: 88r; /Lion's Gate/Photofest: 18bl; /Mielniczek/Dalle: 75l; /Scarlet Page: 91; /Ian Palmer: 48r; / Ed Sirrs: 29tr, 29b, 35; /Ian Tilton: 42, 43; /Alice Wheeler: 20, 21, 22-23, 26, 32

Private Collection: 16bl

Rex/Shutterstock: 14, 63, 67, 68l, 68r, 69, 70r, 79, 91r, 92

Kirk Weddle Photography: 44r

All other Nirvana items supplied by Ross Harkness and photographed by Karl Adamson

Every effort has been made to acknowledge correctly and contact the source and/or copyright holder of each picture and Carlton Books Limited apologises for any unintentional errors or omissions, which will be corrected in future editions of this book.

RIGHT: Dave Grohl, Kurt Cobain and Krist Novoselic: Nirvana in Germany, November 12, 1991.